Praise for *Subscription Marketing*

"Keeping an existing customer is much more profitable than selling a new one, especially in a subscription business. Anne Janzer shows you how to add value and nurture customers before and after the sale, driving success in today's real-time business environment."

David Meerman Scott
Best-selling author of *The New Rules of Marketing and PR* and *Fanocracy*

"Anne's terrific book is an excellent primer to help your business take advantage of the subscription economy, while navigating around potential potholes. And as a bonus: It's clear, straightforward, and refreshingly jargon-free!"

Ann Handley
Chief Content Officer, MarketingProfs, and author of the WSJ best seller, *Everybody Writes*

"Finally, a roadmap. Anne Janzer not only illustrates the power of truly understanding what drives value throughout the subscription customer lifecycle, but essentially gives us the very roadmap needed to make it happen."

Michelle Lange
Cofounder, SUBTA
(Subscription Trade Association)

"Although there is no 'holy grail' measurement for content marketing, there is one that sits atop the rest—the subscriber. As more organizations move from paid to owned media, acquiring and keeping subscribers to our information is more important than ever. Read Anne's book and you'll have everything you need to create and execute a subscription strategy that works."

Joe Pulizzi
Founder, Content Marketing Institute
Author of two best-selling books:
Content Inc. and *Epic Content Marketing*

"We all want customers to stay longer, buy more along the way, expand their relationship with us, and tell their friends and peers about us. And the only reliable way to consistently get those incredibly valuable results is to ensure our customers are continually getting more and more value from their relationship with us. Luckily, Anne's book shows you exactly how to do this."

Lincoln Murphy
Author of *Customer Success*,
Founder of Sixteen Ventures

"Anne Janzer has noticed what many marketers have overlooked: There's a 'silent revolution' taking place as more products and services are being sold on a subscription basis. With the publication of the third edition of *Subscription Marketing*, Anne Janzer goes deeper into the topic with fresh insights, examples, and suggestions for profiting from this proven strategy."

Roger C. Parker
Content Marketing Institute
Top-ranked blogger

"The shift to a subscription economy and the massive competition for consumer attention make it more critical than ever for businesses to build relationships with their customers. In Subscription Marketing, Anne Janzer provides a clear concise guide to building and maintaining those relationships. This book is a must-read for all entrepreneurs as well as marketers!"

Jill Soley
Author of *Beyond Product*

"Customer success teams need account-based marketing strategies to operate at scale. This book will teach you how to develop effective customer campaigns after the sale to increase adoption and growth."

Irit Eizips
Founder, CSM Practice

"Selling into an installed base should be a core component of any Sales/Marketing strategy. And yet it's often overlooked. Janzer's excellent book focuses on this low-hanging fruit and how to leverage it for greater profitability. This book is required reading for anyone trying to maximize their marketing budget—which is everyone."

Tom Hogan
Founder and Principal, Crowded Ocean, coauthor of
The Ultimate Start-Up Guide

"Filled with great examples across industries, this book is a well-written and easy 'must-read' on why and how to add value for both subscriptions and non-subscription-based services alike."

Kathy Klotz-Guest
Founder, Keeping it Human, Inc.
Author of *Stop Boring Me!*

Also by Anne Janzer

The Writer's Process: Getting Your Brain in Gear
The Workplace Writer's Process: Getting the Job Done
Writing to Be Understood: What Works and Why

SUBSCRIPTION MARKETING

STRATEGIES FOR NURTURING CUSTOMERS IN A WORLD OF CHURN

Third Edition

Anne Janzer

Foreword by Robbie Kellman Baxter

Cuesta Park Consulting

Subscription Marketing:
Strategies for Nurturing Customers in a World of Churn
Third Edition

Copyright © 2020 Anne Janzer

Cuesta Park Consulting
San Luis Obispo, California

Printed in the United States of America

ISBNs
Paperback: 978-0-9996248-7-6
Hardcover: 978-0-9996248-8-3
Ebook: 978-0-9996248-6-9

Cover design by Laura Duffy Design

Contents

Foreword

By Robbie Kellman Baxter

Five years ago, when *The Membership Economy* was first published, most organizations didn't realize that subscription pricing or membership models could work for their industries. They would tell me, "I admire what Netflix/Amazon/Salesforce is doing, but it's just not relevant for us."

Fast-forward to today: Everywhere you look, organizations are trying to build forever transactions with the people they serve and prioritizing lifetime customer value over metrics like new customer acquisition or average order size. Businesses of all sizes, in nearly every industry, are discovering that subscription models can be incredibly lucrative—if not a competitive necessity.

But moving to subscriptions isn't easy.

In working with companies including Microsoft, Electronic Arts, the *Wall Street Journal*, and Fitbit, I've seen firsthand the magnitude of changes involved in successfully building customer-centric cultures and processes.

That's why *Subscription Marketing* is so important. Anne looks at subscription business models through the lens of the marketer. And the role of the marketer in a subscription business is very different from what it is in a transactional business. It's less about splashy creative and more about ongoing nurturing, less about growth hacking and more about the customer journey. Marketing a subscription model requires a new set of skills *and* a new mindset.

Anne and I first met several years ago at a subscription conference where we were both speaking. I recognized her at once as a kindred spirit.

We both gravitated to the world of subscriptions because of the way the best subscription organizations put the relationship with the customer at the center. We each recognize the importance of effective communication in any subscription model, not only to drive the moment of transaction, but also to deepen engagement among subscribers.

She has become a close friend and colleague and helped me tremendously as I wrote my second book, *The Forever Transaction*. She is both a subject matter expert and a sophisticated writer, so you're in for a great treat with this new edition.

If you haven't read this book before, you will love how it frames three key ideas:

1. Why this trend is happening now and what it means for the marketer

2. How to develop and deploy the required skills in the subscription tool kit

3. How to apply these skills in *your* organization

If you already have a copy of Anne's book, you'll love the new case studies and frameworks, and the insight she provides on emerging trends affecting practitioners now. And if you're like me, you'll be glad to have a copy that isn't dog-eared and coffee-stained from use.

Robbie Kellman Baxter

Author, *The Membership Economy* and
The Forever Transaction

Preface to the Third Edition

As the author of this book, I feel like I'm involved in a subscription relationship with it. Every two or three years, I renew my investment by bringing it up to date. The book before you is the third edition.

Why do I keep renewing this book?

Like any loyal subscriber, I re-up my subscription because of the value of the experience. This book changed my career, setting me on a new path. Revising and updating this book gives me the chance to reconnect with people I admire, to follow up on stories, and to revisit the examples to learn which ones have endured.

Second, as a subscription marketer, I'm committed to delivering and sustaining value. For this topic, sustaining value means updating the book to reflect the world around us.

And *wow,* has that world changed since the first edition was published in January 2015. Here are a few key trends.

The Subscription Economy is now the mainstream economy.

Back in 2015, I encountered many quizzical looks. Subscription marketing? Is this book about selling magazines and newspapers?

Today, I don't have to convince people of the importance of the subscription model. You already understand, because you see it every day. You can subscribe to the clothes you wear, the cosmetics or toiletries you use daily, and the meals you make for dinner. In the evenings, you settle into the couch while Disney, Apple, and Netflix compete for your streaming video business.

This is true around the globe. *Subscription Marketing* has been translated into Japanese and Korean, and I hear from people in many countries about their businesses.

More organizations are adopting subscriptions models.

The first edition targeted the people I had worked with for years: marketers in large technology companies. But it reached a broader audience despite my targeting. In large companies, Customer Success teams were among the first to welcome the ideas in this book. Small businesses and entrepreneurs embraced the book. This topic is nearly universal.

My opinions have clarified.

After years of speaking with marketers, entrepreneurs, and industry thought leaders, I have refined my definition of subscription marketing. At the outset, I focused on tactics and strategies. Today I realize that mindset is as important, if not more so, than the tactics you deploy.

This third edition in your hands reflects those changes. It spends less time on the basics of subscription business models; you can find excellent guidance in other books. (See the suggested reading list in the Resources area on my website at AnneJanzer.com.) Other changes include the following:

- Part One now features a short but critical chapter on the concepts of trust and value—true marketing imperatives in the Subscription Economy.

- The value nurturing examples in Part Two have been updated and expanded.

- Part Three includes new chapters focused on start-ups seeking fast growth; small businesses and solopreneurs; and large, established businesses.

I am confident that you'll find practices and suggestions you can use in your business, no matter what industry you're in or how large your enterprise. And I hope the ideas you find here resonate with your own experience as a full participant in the Subscription Economy.

- Continuing to nurture and enhance the customer's experience of value long after the sale
- Forming long-lasting customer relationships that inspire loyalty and advocacy in the subscriber base

Traditional marketing strategies and techniques focus on leading people to the initial sale, turning prospects into customers. Subscription businesses shift their focus from the point of sale to the long-term, ongoing customer relationship. The subscriber remains a prospect, deserving ongoing engagement and nurturing.

> In the Subscription Economy, you're only doing half of your job as a marketer if you focus on the sale and ignore the customer.

If your business depends on subscription-based relationships with your customers, then it's time to adopt the mindset and strategies of subscription marketing.

What Is Subscription Marketing, Anyway?

I've struggled to come up with a concise working definition of *subscription marketing*, partly because *marketing* is such a vague, misunderstood term. (My mother is convinced it means "sales.") Then I heard Jill Soley, a strategic product and marketing leader and coauthor of *Beyond Product*, define marketing as "two-way communication between your company and your customers."

Aha! That works for me. So, with permission from Soley, let's define subscription marketing as follows:

Subscription Marketing is two-way communication between your company and customers in a subscription relationship, with the purpose of sustaining the value of that relationship for both parties.

While this book focuses on marketing after the sale (which I call *value nurturing*), those activities are part of a broader shift in the marketing discipline. Subscription marketing is marketing with a long-term perspective. It's changing your mindset to focus on the relationship rather than revenue alone. It's looking beyond lead generation to cultivating both trust and value, before and after the point of conversion.

Subscription marketing resets fundamental ideas you may have about marketing. For example, as a subscription marketer:

- Leads are fine. Relationships are better.
- Large marketing budgets are helpful. Creativity is priceless.
- Interrupt-driven tactics like advertising deliver inconsistent results. Adding value always works.
- Chasing sales is exhausting. Creating value, however, is energizing.

Subscription marketing doesn't technically require a subscription revenue model. All you need is a shift in mindset. But if you *have* a subscription model and want to achieve long-term success, you need to adopt the practices of subscription marketing.

Part One

The Subscription Shift

subscription, through valuable content, instant gratification, and convenience. (You'll read about these practices in Part Two.)

- *Valuable content*: Prime members can access free streaming videos, Kindle books, Audible channels, and music.

- *Instant gratification*: In addition to the two-day shipping that defines Prime, sometimes Prime members can get free *two-hour* shipping with Amazon Prime Now.

- *Convenience*: If getting off the couch and going to the computer is too much effort, use the Prime Now app on your phone. Get local restaurants to bring dinner to your door with Amazon Restaurants.

Amazon has filed a patent for *anticipatory shipping*— shipping stuff before you actually order it. Keep an eye on what this giant retailer is doing.

Subscription Boxes

The big subscription activity in retail is happening inside the box. Subscription box companies curate and ship collections of related goods, often hoping you will purchase follow-up versions of the items you like.

A growing community of subscription box companies offer a wide range of goods, including:

      3D printing supplies

      Air travel

Chickens (oddly, there are several subscription chicken offers—you might say, even, a flock of them)

Co-living spaces

Cosmetics and beauty product samples

Food, meal-planning, and ready-to-prepare meals

Gaming gear

Hot sauce

Juice cleanse regimens

Pet food, supplies, and toys

Running gear

Toys

Underwear

Professional Services

We are accustomed to ongoing subscriptions for repeat services like gardening, pool maintenance, and cleaning. For other professional services, we expect to pay as we need them, with hourly or one-time fees.

Many of those providers, however, are expanding their business models with online subscriptions. A quick web search uncovers a wide range of professional services:

- Accounting (Bench)
- Corporate recruitment services (Ascend HR Corp. profiled later)
- Financial planning (LearnVest)
- Legal advice (Rocket Lawyer)

- Physician house calls (NetMedNow)
- Therapy (Talkspace)

Industrial Goods as Subscription Services

Established vendors in business-to-business markets are adding value and building recurring revenue streams through *managed services* models. A managed service combines equipment and services as a subscription. The service provider retains ownership of any equipment, while managing and maintaining it on behalf of the customer.

Printer manufacturers like Xerox and HP offer managed print services to business clients, helping them scope and then meet their printing needs, campus by campus. Services include everything from maintenance to stocking supplies. Customers pay for the number of pages printed.

How about industrial chemicals? Should businesses actually *own* the chemicals they use, or might they simply pay for the processes provided by that chemical? Using chemical leasing (or *chemical management services*), chemical manufacturers and distributors work with industrial customers to determine their objectives, then supply and manage the appropriate chemicals for the task at hand.

Suppliers are compensated for the *effectiveness* of their chemicals, not the volumes they sell. From an environmental perspective, everyone benefits by doing critical processes with fewer chemicals. The service providers have the necessary knowledge to handle and dispose of the chemicals safely and responsibly.

Want to try 3D printing without investing in the device yet? You can subscribe to an advance 3D printer from Carbon. In addition to the device, you'll get support services that help you test the possibilities of 3D printing in your business.

The Internet of Things

My car sent me an email the other day. At least, that's what it felt like. I got an email reporting the mileage and condition of the car's systems. It's not enough that *we* spend all of our time online; now our vehicles and appliances do as well.

The term *Internet of Things* (IoT) refers to the growing number of devices with embedded network connectivity. It's all around us: a watch nudging you to stand up, a thermostat tracking your presence, or a remote industrial site self-reporting an anomalous reading. The Internet of Things grows larger with each passing day.

The Internet of Things opens up the possibility for manufacturers to offer subscription-based services alongside the devices they sell. Devices like smart thermostats (Nest), wearable fitness technologies (Fitbit and others), and solar panels all have their own apps.

Initially, IoT vendors make most of their revenue from the sale of the device itself. In a world of networked appliances, the real value to the business is not the one-time sale, but the ongoing relationship and data gathered through mobile or web-based applications. For example, Peloton offers a digital subscription to live and recorded classes, while Fitbit offers both free and paid versions of its fitness apps.

The subscription relationship is an essential component of the Internet of Things.

We Are All Participants in the Subscription Economy

If you think your industry cannot be disrupted by subscriptions, you're not thinking hard enough.

Perhaps your core product or services won't fit a subscription billing model—some products and services never will. But that doesn't mean you should dispense with the subscription marketing practices of building long-term relationships with subscribers. Why? Your customers are all living in this subscription world.

Have you ever heard the saying "A rising tide lifts all boats"? Rising customer expectations affect all businesses.

No matter what industry you're in, your customers live and operate in this emerging and evolving Subscription Economy. Even if you're in the Business-to-Business (B2B) market, selling to organizations, the individuals you deal with interact with successful subscription companies in their personal lives.

The person who is delighted by the personalized video they receive when signing up for a service may feel put off by a form letter that begins, "Dear valued customer…" Having had a taste of meaningful relationships, they'll sour on stale transactions.

The rising subscription tide raises all customer expectations. If you don't adjust, you may just find yourself under water.

Chapter 2

Shifting to Subscriptions

If a subscription isn't already part of your business model, you may be adding one soon. This chapter offers a brief survey of ways to make the subscription shift in your business.

One size does *not* fit all organizations. By considering a range of options, you will find the path that makes the most sense for your purposes. If your business is already subscription-based, you may find inspiration for expanding your offerings.

This chapter is not meant to be a guide to shifting business models. For an in-depth discussion and step-by-step playbook on the move to subscriptions, read Robbie Kellman Baxter's *The Forever Transaction*.

Shifting to Subscription-Based Billing for Existing Companies

If you sell products or services through one-time transactions, you may want to change your revenue model. You have many options. Common adoption models include:

- The subscription trial
- The segmented approach
- The "all-in" pivot

We'll take a quick tour through the advantages and challenges of each approach.

The Subscription Trial

Cautious companies may give the subscription model a trial run without changing existing offerings or processes.

While this seems like a relatively low-risk approach, the inherent lack of commitment may doom the trial to failure. In fear of cannibalizing revenues, salespeople may not push the subscription. Without investing in an onboarding process that guides subscribers to rapid success, you may experience high churn rates as customers fail to renew.

The financial results of a short trial may be underwhelming, since it takes time for subscription revenues to accumulate. Disappointing revenues from a subscription product confirm the skeptic's hypothesis that a subscription model doesn't fit the market. Failure becomes a self-fulfilling prophecy. You'll hear rationalizations like "*Our* buyers aren't interested in subscriptions" or "That doesn't work for what *we* do."

Complacency can be dangerous in competitive markets.

Give the subscription model a fair trial by allowing enough time and committing resources. Experiment with the subscription offer itself. For example:

- Do you take everything you offer and lump it as a subscription?

- Could you package one small part of your total portfolio as a recurring subscription to reach a broader market?

- Could you create an entirely new subscription service that expands your potential market or offers additional value to existing customers?

Develop a solution that aligns with your core value proposition and market needs. Make sure you understand the customer's reason for subscribing. If you simply change a pricing model without adding value through the subscription, existing customers may feel like they're being played. Make sure that there's something compelling about your subscription offer, other than what people can get by simply purchasing repeatedly through one-time transactions.

I've spoken with people who told me, "We tried a subscription and it didn't work for us." It turns out, they'd tried rolling all of their current offerings into a monthly billing cycle, without thinking about how to add value or how subscribing is different from purchasing. It's not just about pricing.

Segmenting with Subscriptions

Selling the same product with different pricing and delivery models presents challenges for your sales team. You might target a specific market segment using a subscription model, then dedicate marketing and customer success efforts to that segment. Using this approach, you can develop targeted value propositions for the distinct markets.

A few years back, I worked with a company that sold on-premises identity and access management software to large institutional clients. The company then developed a cloud-based offering to target the small and mid-sized business market. The subscription offering let them address a new market with software-as-a-service.

Over time, the packaged software became a secondary offering, but its revenues supported the transition. Segmenting the customer base was key to this company's subscription shift.

Using a subscription model can serve as a useful test case for a market segment. Eventually, you may have to decide which model will get most of your development and marketing effort going forward. At that point, you might execute a *subscription pivot.*

The Subscription Pivot

In October 2011, Adobe launched Creative Cloud® as a subscription, cloud-based version of its packaged design software. But it didn't pivot right away: Adobe maintained both subscription and packaged versions of the software for more than a year, until announcing it would no longer update the packaged software.

According to Adobe's press release announcing the shift on May 6, 2013, the decision was about accelerating the pace of innovation in its software:

Focusing development on Creative Cloud will not only accelerate the rate at which Adobe can innovate but also broaden the type of innovation the company can offer the creative community.

The press and investors complained. Shifting revenues to a recurring model inevitably means a short-term revenue drop before long-term growth. But the company stayed on course, expanding its software-as-a-service commitment with Adobe Marketing Cloud and Document Cloud.

It's worked out well for Adobe. In the 2018 fiscal year, the company realized over $9 billion in revenue—a record figure that represented 24 percent year-over-year growth. Over $5 billion of that comes from subscriptions. Patience and a firm commitment paid off, and Adobe's investors are convinced.

Subscriptions as a Marketing Strategy

In certain situations, the subscription model doesn't *threaten* existing business models—it supports and enhances them. Subscription offerings can drive demand for existing, one-time offerings or strengthen customer loyalty.

Online retailers have discovered that adding a subscription can increase sales of products outside the subscription. It reduces the customer's psychological pain of paying by lumping multiple purchase decisions into a single decision to subscribe. Plus, subscriptions are a real convenience for many people.

A subscription can also function as a cross-selling offer to existing customers. Traditional retailers that add a curated monthly "box" subscription expose their customers to new products while strengthening the relationship.

For example, a growing number of companies offer subscriptions to monthly boxes of cosmetics and beauty supply samples. Subscribers pay for the fun of discovery, then order more of the products they love. The subscription purchase drives further sales.

Or consider Amazon Prime, which is only one of the massive retailer's subscription offerings. Amazon Prime members pay $119 per year for free two-day shipping for eligible goods, along with a host of other goodies. Amazon is experimenting with free one-day shipping, to further sweeten the deal.

The expedited shipping costs Amazon significant money. But Amazon makes the money back in other ways. Prime members purchase more from Amazon than non-Prime members; Morgan Stanley says that Prime members spend on average $2,486 per year, compared to $700 for the non-Prime Amazon shopper. Amazon makes back that money it spends on free shipping. In its annual report, Amazon calls Amazon Prime an effective worldwide marketing tool.

What Happens Behind the Scenes During the Shift

A subscription model affects various parts of your business, including sales, finance, research and development, and customer success. Whether you are changing business models or adding subscriptions to your menu of offerings, you must answer some difficult questions, such as:

- How do you sell subscriptions alongside another sales model?
- How do you compensate salespeople?
- Who handles renewals?
- Do you recognize revenues when the customer makes a commitment, or at the conclusion of the subscription time period?
- Does the same solution messaging apply across all business models?
- Can you address a different part of the market with the subscription model? Should you develop different customer personas?
- How do you price the subscription to support long-term business growth?

Transitioning to subscriptions can be difficult. Old ways of doing things don't work well. If you don't adjust to these differences, you may not experience the revenue growth you expect.

The subscription model may bring unexpected *benefits* beyond the obvious ones of predictable revenue streams and long-term customer relationships. These include:

Competitive differentiation: If you are the first in your market to offer subscriptions, the model can be a significant advantage. With a steady eye on subscriber usage and churn, you may be more attuned and responsive to market changes than competitors that sell once and walk away.

Market expansion: Subscriptions may open new market opportunities by making your solutions accessible and reducing the entry price point.

Unexpected benefits: Adobe struggled for many years with people using pirated copies of its software, particularly for costly Creative Cloud applications like Photoshop. The subscription model automatically reduces piracy, since the company no longer ships packaged software that can be copied. Further, organizations on tight budgets with single projects can pay to use the service for only a month or two.

For an example of the organization-wide impact of changing business models, let's look at the story of one service business that made the switch.

A Case Study: Pioneering a Subscription Model in Recruiting

When Houston-based Ascend HR Corporation made a shift to subscription services, it ended up reframing fundamental practices in the recruiting industry and entirely transforming its own business.

Most outsourced recruiting firms charge clients per placement (a *contingency* pricing model). Companies hire the firms to find people for difficult-to-fill executive or technical positions and pay a fee for each successful hire.

The traditional fee-for-hire model often puts the hiring company and recruiting agency in conflict with each other. If the hiring company fills a position independently, it avoids paying the recruiter's fee. Recruiters and their clients *compete* for the hire.

Several years ago, Rollis Fontenot III, president of Ascend HR, decided to offer placement services as a monthly or annual subscription rather pricing per hire. The new service,

HR Maximizer, provided recruiting services for a monthly fee, with unlimited hires. With this model, everyone works toward the same objective: finding the right people for the open positions.

As a trailblazer in this space, Fontenot had few models for his transition. He says, "We didn't know where HR Maximizer was going to lead. We had no template, no starting point. We determined pricing levels and service offerings by trial and error. We've learned to simplify and clarify our offerings as much as possible."

This model has been so successful that Fontenot split off HR Maximizer Inc into its own company, which accounts for most of Ascend HR's revenues. HR Maximizer now exclusively serves clients in the healthcare industry, where recruiting is a constant challenge. The company has expanded its geographic reach beyond Texas. And with high client retention, the average customer lifetime value of each client has increased and revenues are predictable. Fontenot says, "By running HR Maximizer as a separate entity, we're able to see how profitable it is compared to our old business model."

The subscription model expanded the range of potential services Ascend HR can offer to clients. Today the company focuses on attracting candidates through a range of services, including videos with hiring managers and clinical staff as well as managing live events with social media influencers. They are also working with chatbots and artificial intelligence to streamline the job inquiry and application processes.

The result is a work environment that is not only profitable, but creative and fun. Fontenot says, "We were in a holding pattern with the contingency business. We enjoy this a lot more. The learning curve hasn't been straightforward, but the subscription business model is paying for our education and giving us a chance to experiment and find new ways to serve our clients."

Chapter 3

What This Means for Marketers

Subscriptions change the nature of the relationship between your business and its customers. That fact should transform the way you approach marketing.

For example, what does it mean to you that your business's revenue model is changing? How is the role of marketing shifting and evolving in successful subscription businesses? Do subscriptions make marketing more or less relevant to the business?

Let's look at the ramifications of subscriptions for the traditional practices of marketing.

Follow the Money

Most dedicated marketers feel their work is important. Yet surprisingly few track their effect on overall business performance and revenues.

Historically, the role of marketing in large organizations has been to attract customers or deliver prospects to a sales team, with the expectation that some percentage of those leads turn into revenue. Particularly in business-to-business (B2B) companies, marketers focus on generating leads, nurturing prospects, and enabling sales. For many years, that commitment has served businesses well.

A subscription revenue model uncouples revenue from the point of sale.

Subscription offerings have lower up-front prices than one-time sales because customers pay as they go. Over time, if the subscriber remains a customer, the *lifetime value* of that relationship grows, even before cross-sell or upsell activities.

The longer you stay in business with a subscription model, the more of your revenues shift to a recurring model—*if* your customers stick around. If you focus only on the moment of the sale, you're missing the bigger picture.

> To remain relevant as a subscription marketer, follow the revenues and focus on what happens after the moment of conversion.

Marketers who don't take action risk falling into the *marketing-revenue gap*. They spend their time and resources on one part of the revenue stream (net new revenues), while long-term business success depends on the current customer base (recurring revenues).

To avoid the gap, look past the traditional lead-generation and lead-nurturing activities, and beyond the traditional scope of the marketing organization.

To shift your marketing mindset, start by questioning the "funnel" metaphor.

Rethink the Funnel

Every marketer has the image of the sales and marketing funnel imprinted in their minds. It's a linear, one-way path that fields potential prospects and feeds them through campaigns and content until the glorious moment of conversion: the sale.

For most marketers, the rest of the customer's experience is out of sight, out of mind. We spend all of our time and attention on "top of funnel" (or TOFU) activities and "feeding the funnel."

The funnel metaphor has serious problems. First, it oversimplifies the process of sales, particularly in a world in which prospective customers do initial research independently, outside of the organization's awareness. The funnel treats the sales process as an inevitable, linear path filled with passive customers. Reality is rarely so simple.

The metaphor also discounts the processes *after* the sale. It ignores other feedback loops built into the subscription marketing process, such as:

- Nurturing customers so that they renew
- Selling more offerings to existing subscribers
- Soliciting customer referrals, which arrive as new leads

Many marketing leaders have proposed modifications to the funnel, tweaking the metaphor to fit into an hourglass or adding "bottom of funnel" activities. My problem is with the metaphor itself. We all know what a basic funnel looks like: wide at the top and skinny at the bottom.

If you add after-the-sale feedback loops onto the traditional funnel image, you end up with something that looks more like a French horn—an instrument that is notoriously difficult to master.

Ultimately, the staying power of the funnel metaphor imperils marketing's ongoing relationship with the customer. Because the current customers have traveled beyond the critical part of the funnel (conversion), they seem less relevant to marketers. Our processes, priorities, and budgets are skewed toward brand recognition and lead generation.

If you accept that existing customers are critical to subscription revenue and business growth, then you also must accept that the initial sale is not the endpoint in a subscription business. It's just a beginning.

In the subscription model, the sales process has significant feedback loops. It's no longer a linear, one-way path. A *customer journey* is a better metaphor for today's marketing and sales environment.

The customer journey describes the steps a person takes when interacting with your company and solution. The journey metaphor puts that person's *experience* at the center of attention, not their status with your company. The customer is an active participant in a journey, rather than an inanimate object traveling through a funnel.

To engage with the customer journey, marketing organizations must understand how their solutions fit in customers' lives, from where they look for answers to problems to how they buy and use things.

And the customer's journey doesn't end with the purchase. Once subscribers start using the solution, it either meets their requirements or doesn't. Then they face fresh challenges, or things change. In a B2B context, the customer's business may grow or shift. Life goes on after the purchase.

Whether or not your business remains part of that ongoing story depends, in part, on what you do after the sale. To track marketing effectiveness in this new, after-the-funnel world, you must work with new metrics.

Learn New Metrics

Savvy, revenue-relevant marketers understand the financial impact of the marketing investment beyond net new sales. To determine where to invest effort and resources for a subscription business, ask these questions:

- How much does it cost to move a customer through the sales process, accounting for marketing and sales activities? (That's the average *customer acquisition cost*, or CAC.)

- How much revenue do you realize from the average customer (*average revenue per account*, or ARPA)?

- How much does it cost to serve that customer?

- Given the cost of serving the customer, how long does it take the subscription customer to repay the cost of acquisition and become profitable? (That's the *payback period*.) How many renewal cycles must pass?

- How long does the average customer remain and renew?

- How many subscribers leave each month (the *monthly customer churn*)?

Accounting for the costs of acquisition and operations, a subscription customer is rarely profitable when they first sign up, even if they pay for a year up front. If you spend $100 to acquire a customer and the subscription fee is $5 per month, then a subscriber must remain a paying customer for twenty months to recoup acquisition costs alone. That time frame doesn't include the operational costs of serving the customer.

Your payback period may be a few months or a few years. If it's long, then you'll need to work hard to retain customers past the point of payback.

This has important ramifications for marketing. *Doing a great job raking in new leads may lose money in the long term by attracting the wrong customers.*

This leads us to another critical concept for subscription marketers.

Not All Customers Are Created Equal

In a traditional, one-time-sales model, it didn't matter if you sold a product to someone who wasn't a great fit. They might return it, but usually they didn't.

In a subscription model, it *does* matter if subscribers stick around. Remember that it can take several renewal cycles for a customer to pay back the costs of acquisition and service.

Rather than focusing on *how many* leads you generate, consider how to attract the prospects who will find success with the solution and remain loyal customers. You may have to give up the thrill of running massive lead-generating campaigns and focus instead on fewer, highly targeted prospects.

To find the best-converting customers who stick around, pay attention to the behavior of your most successful customers. Then, figure out how to change your marketing practices to attract more people like them.

- Identify target customer segments and profiles (or personas) that are a good fit.

- Identify the stages in the customer journey for those personas.

- Provide content and support at each phase of the journey, from initial awareness to the customer's long-term experience.

> In the Subscription Economy, you are just getting started when someone becomes a customer.

The demise of the funnel and the emergence of subscription relationships bring opportunities to tell stories and engage with customers, and to forge an expanded role for marketing.

Once you have scrapped the funnel, mapped out the customer journey, and learned the right metrics, it's time to rework your marketing campaigns and strategies to reflect this approach. As you craft those marketing practices, focus on the guiding principles of trust and value. That's the subject of the next chapter.

Chapter 4

Cultivate Trust and Value

As you reset your priorities to adjust to the realities of subscription marketing, you might wonder where to begin and what to do differently.

Fortunately, subscription marketing builds on existing marketing skills and activities. If you routinely create great content, you'll keep doing more of the same. If you can tell a compelling story that differentiates your business from the competition, you're well on your way.

Now use those skills to get the *right* people to sign up—the ones who will stick around—and then keep nurturing them. With every campaign, focus on how you can build and sustain *trust and value* in your subscription relationships.

As marketing expert and author David Meerman Scott writes in *Fanocracy*, "The relationships we build with our customers are more important than the products and services we sell to them."

The New Marketing Imperatives: Trust and Value

A subscription isn't a financial transaction—it's an ongoing relationship. Any marriage counselor will tell you that successful relationships involve trust in both directions.

Subscribers trust that you will deliver, that you won't misuse their data, and that your billing practices are ethical. They must believe that you won't try to rip them off or trap them in a relationship they cannot leave.

The business must trust its subscribers as well. You are accepting less revenue up front in the hope of a longer-term relationship. You may not recover the entire cost of acquiring a customer on the initial signup. You're absorbing financial risk. You count on that subscriber acting in good faith, and hope they will remain long enough, at least, to recover the costs of acquiring and serving them.

Value is also a two-way street. Your product/service is worth something to your subscribers, and those subscribers have value for your business. The value of a customer to the business grows over time if the customer values the experience of being a customer.

Trust and value: These are your guides to subscription marketing. Let's look at how they factor into marketing activities before the sale and afterward.

Subscription Marketing Before the Sale

Most of this book concerns what happens after the sale. Yet you still need to generate demand for your solutions. The subscription relationship changes the focus of your demand-generation activities in two ways:

Better targeting. Customers who leave shortly after signing up will consume your marketing budget without generating long-term revenue. Rather than going wide with your marketing efforts, focus on finding those people who represent the best fit for your business. You'll be much better off with a smaller number of great-fit leads than a large number of so-so ones.

Trustworthy behavior. In addition to selling people on the features and benefits of the solution, you also need to earn their trust. Cheesy, high-pressure sales tactics backfire in a subscription-based business. Storytelling, brand perception, and authentic values help you earn initial trust.

> Before the sale, subscription marketers demonstrate value and earn trust.

After the Sale: Still Trust and Value

Although the work of the subscription marketer continues after the moment of conversion or signup, your tactics may shift. The messaging you use to generate demand may not resonate with those who have already joined or subscribed.

Before the sale, you must motivate people to take the positive action to change. After the sale, you want to encourage them to stay and feel good about their decision.

You may pitch different features or benefits after the signup, since the person's situation has changed by becoming a customer. Your ideal user may subscribe because of one specific need, then remain loyal because they have become part of a community, or because they enjoy interacting with your business.

Your task after the conversion is twofold:

1. Sustain the trust that the subscriber has granted you.
4. Nurture and support the customer's perception of value, so they continue to renew, and perhaps increase their spending with you.

After the conversion, marketing's role is to nurture value and sustain trust.

Marketing isn't the only group on the hook for these objectives. Marketing may set the tone and expectations, but the relationship exists between your customer and your entire company. Demonstrating value and sustaining trust requires cooperation among marketing, customer success, customer support, sales, service, and other groups.

> Marketing creates the promise. The whole business fulfills it.

The processes and campaigns that nurture customer experience have many labels, including customer advocacy, retention, and customer marketing. We'll group all these activities under the broader term of "customer value nurturing," or more simply, *value nurturing*. This is the subject of the next chapter.

Chapter 5

Value Nurturing

Beginning golfers are taught to work on their *entire* swing, including the follow-through. The follow-through on a golf swing affects where the ball goes once you hit it. Value nurturing is like the follow-through for marketing and sales, ensuring that customers continue on the course you want them to travel.

Before the initial sale, you find prospects through thought leadership and lead generation. Lead-nurturing activities convince prospects of the potential value they can get from your solution. If you succeed, the prospect becomes a customer. *Value nurturing* is the marketing follow-through for that activity.

> Value nurturing is the act of supporting the customer's experience of value.

Once the sale is complete, other parts of the organization come into play, but marketing still plays a significant role. Marketing can set customers on the path to achieving the functional or financial results they expected from signing up. Marketing can gently nudge customers to *recognize* that they are succeeding. And creative marketers add value *outside* the solution, through content, community, additional services, or the quality of the relationship experienced by the customer.

Value nurturing turns customers into loyal or repeat customers, and successful customers into advocates.

There's nothing revolutionary about the idea of marketing to current customers. You might think that I'm stating the obvious. But in observing the practices of many businesses, I often feel that customers are neglected. Some marketing organizations treat "customer marketing" as a backwater, *not* where the creative and visible campaigns happen. This mindset must change.

Subscription customers deserve renewed marketing attention. For that reason, I suggest creating a new label—*value nurturing*—that identifies marketing activities after the sale as being of equal importance to generating and nurturing new leads.

Many business activities belong under the value-nurturing umbrella:

- **Customer success management**: Today this term is associated with a function that lives either in support or sales, but rarely in marketing. Yet to scale up customer success efforts across tens of thousands of customers, you have to deploy marketing campaigns. Value nurturing is customer success executed at scale.

- **Customer retention:** Most customer retention efforts focus on finding customers at risk of leaving and convincing them to stay. The term typically applies to solving problems rather than creating value.
- **Upselling and cross-selling:** These are important results of successful value nurturing, but never mistake *selling* for creating value.

Value nurturing takes place after lead generation, lead nurturing, and customer conversion. It is the next logical step in subscription marketing.

The word *value* has inherent ambiguity, which works well. Consider common meanings of the word:

1. Value (*verb*): to consider something or someone as important or useful. (Shakespeare: "I was too young that time to value her, but now I know her.")
2. Value (*noun*): a relative assessment of worth or importance. ("What's the value of this painting?")
3. Value (*noun*): a principle or standard of behavior. (Gandhi: "Your habits become your values, your values become your destiny.")

Value nurturing can confirm the customer's belief that the ongoing subscription is a smart economic decision. Marketing can also increase the customer's perception of the relative value of a solution over time. These activities reinforce the first two definitions of *value*.

Last but not least, marketing may also align the solution with the customer's personal values (definition #3). Many people are interested in doing business with organizations that share their core beliefs. This fact is spurring a growth in purpose-driven marketing related to social or environmental issues.

This third meaning, the alignment of principles or ideals, carries particular weight in the Subscription Economy because the customer maintains an ongoing relationship with the business, and shared values strengthen relationships.

Whose Value Is It, Anyway?

It's tempting to associate value nurturing with monetary metrics such as *customer lifetime value*. How much money does the customer contribute to the business during their relationship? How can you optimize that?

Revenue growth is, of course, your objective. But if you approach value nurturing purely with the thought of getting more money from existing customers, you're likely to get it wrong. We've all experienced a poorly executed upsell at least once in our lives and realize that it damages the customer relationship.

Your customers can tell when you're interested in them only for the money, not the relationship.

Value nurturing is about increasing the *customer's* perceived value from the solution, not wringing every dollar out of the customer. The better you are at making your customers successful, the more successful your business will be over the long run.

> Revenue growth is the natural result of value nurturing done well.

Consider another metric: Economic Value to the Customer (EVC). Economists speak of this number as the maximum that a customer will pay for a solution. EVC is the sum of *tangible* and *intangible* benefits to the customer. For a subscription customer, the EVC must exceed the cost of renewing. Marketing's job is to increase the economic value as experienced by the customer.

Lest we let the economists have the last word, cognitive science suggests that the potential for customer happiness is built into the subscription business model itself.

Paying causes us psychological pain. We do not enjoy losses, and the moment of paying seems like a loss. (No surprise here.) A subscription replaces many small decisions to pay with one decision—the subscription.

Cognitive science also tells us that once the pain of payment is done, we are free to enjoy the results of our purchase. In the book *Happy Money: The Science of Happier Spending*, authors Elizabeth Dunn and Michael Norton posit that we are happiest when we pay for something up front and then continue to enjoy it afterward. For example, once you've paid for an all-inclusive vacation, you will likely savor and enjoy every moment.

A subscription model in which you pay up front opens the door for sustained enjoyment. Value nurturing is about optimizing and engineering the post-sale experience of value. It's a quest for customer happiness, and it can be a great deal of fun if you approach it creatively.

The Five Big Ideas of Value Nurturing

Just as the word *value* has several meanings, there are at least five distinct approaches to value nurturing.

1. Helping customers find success

People subscribe to your solution for a reason. Maybe they believe it will save them money or make their lives easier. Perhaps it seems entertaining. They expect value in exchange for subscribing, whether for personal or business use.

The simplest and purest expression of value nurturing is to help your customers realize this value, fulfilling the implicit brand promise of your marketing.

To do this, you may reach beyond the marketing organization, aligning with *customer success management* efforts in the business. Smart subscription marketers are interested in *all* post-sale customer conversations and experiences.

2. Demonstrating value

Once customers start achieving success, marketing can discreetly remind them of the value they're realizing. These strategies range from sending gentle reminders to delivering personalized data. All share the aim of reinforcing the experience of value (tangible and intangible) in the customer's mind.

3. Creating value outside the solution

Creative marketing organizations go beyond merely communicating solution benefits. They add value outside the product or service through content, community, and data. Create entertaining videos, build customer communities, or deliver regular newsletters and courses that help your customers, and you'll make the experience of being a customer richer.

4. Creating value through the relationship

Some businesses are a joy to interact with, with excellent support and thoughtful transactions. Marketing organizations can take ownership of tending and nurturing ongoing relationships with subscribers.

5. Aligning with customer values

Customer loyalty is critical for the financial performance of a subscription-based business, so taking the high road can pay off over time. Businesses that share their customers' values create strong, long-lasting bonds with their customers. Purpose-driven marketing strategies may have growing impact in the years to come.

Choose Your Own Path

The chapters in Part Two present an extensive menu of ideas you can implement for value nurturing. Some belong squarely in the marketing domain, while others require collaboration across organizational boundaries. You may implement many of them quickly and easily; a few require high-level buy-in.

What you do with these strategies is up to you. You may already do many of these activities, though viewing them as *value nurturing* may change your perspective. If you're practicing a few of these strategies, consider adding more. You probably won't reach a saturation point on customer loyalty.

The final chapter in Part Two discusses free trials. For many businesses, the free trial is a critical moment when lead nurturing ends and value nurturing begins. If you offer a free trial, pay attention to whether you're nurturing the customer experience.

The examples that follow come from all types of businesses, not just those with a subscription-based model. Consumer brands like Coca-Cola and rock stars like Lady Gaga alike recognize the value of maintaining audience loyalty. Subscription marketers can learn from many teachers. Pay attention to the experiences of companies outside your own industry. If you market business-to-business solutions, read the consumer-based examples carefully. You can learn a great deal by looking farther afield than your own competition and keeping an open mind. In today's fast-changing marketing environment, stepping outside your comfort zone can yield results.

Part Two

Value-Nurturing Strategies

Chapter 6

Create a Customer Launch Plan

There's nothing most marketers love more than a good launch. A product launch, a company launch, a book launch—you name it, we'll launch it. A launch gives us a sense of accomplishment and an excuse for a party.

In all the excitement about the glamorous, high-profile launches, it's easy to neglect the many small but critical events happening all around you—customer launches. Over time, the cumulative effect of these individual beginnings has a larger impact on your business than any media launch event.

If you're looking for the low-hanging fruit of value-nurturing strategies, you've found it. *Something* motivated the person to become a customer. Do what you can to guide people to ongoing success before they lose momentum and forget why they signed up.

Creating a customer launch plan makes sense for almost any business and works equally well for subscription-based and traditional business models. There's almost no excuse not to have a customer launch plan. Plus, there are powerful psychological reasons for taking action right away.

Design the launch plan to get customers working with and realizing value from your solution as quickly as possible. An early success feeds the *positive confirmation bias*, or our tendency to seek evidence to support the decisions we have already made.

Immediately after making a choice, we look for signs to confirm that the decision was a good one. As behavioral economist Richard Thaler writes in *Misbehaving: The Making of Behavioral Economics*, "People have a natural tendency to search for confirming rather than disconfirming evidence."

We look for those experiences that prove us right in choosing to subscribe. The early days of a subscription are a valuable opportunity to supply that confirming evidence.

That's why the "customer onboarding" or welcome experience is so critical. The first interactions confirm that we made a sound decision to use the service. Because making decisions takes effort, we'd rather not analyze them repeatedly. If we experience good initial results, we will consider the decision a success and are less likely to churn.

Polish the Virtual Packaging

Have you ever wondered why Apple invests so heavily in packaging design for its products? From the moment you open the box, you sense you are using something special. That perception colors your experience going forward.

You may not be shipping products in a box, but your initial interactions with customers are the metaphorical equivalent. Pay attention to the details of how your customers unwrap and explore the experience.

Treat every email, every transaction, and each bit of communication as an opportunity to reinforce the reasons for choosing your business. Work on the packaging for this new relationship. The customer journey does not end at the sale; rather, the point of sale is where the story gets interesting, at least from the customer's perspective.

For example, whenever you subscribe to an application or email service, you inevitably see a message like: "Check your email for a confirmation link." In the United States, this double opt-in ensures that email subscriptions meet anti-spam regulations. It protects the business by validating that the person signing up for the service is associated with the email account being claimed.

What does that opt-in confirmation email look like to subscribers? What is the tone and style? Do you anticipate any problems that people may have? Where do you send them when they click the link to confirm the subscription? What's the first thing a new customer is likely to want to see?

Walk through the process of signing up as if you were a new customer. Look for every opportunity to create the right impression and guide the customer to the next step.

The Welcome Email or Video

Your launch plan might be as simple as a well-constructed welcome email. You *do* have one, right?

I must confess: I sometimes sign up for applications in the heat of the moment, and then don't get started with them. I may forget that I have signed up. A well-written welcome email can save the day.

When I signed up for the Haiku Deck service for creating online presentations, I wasn't actually working on a presentation. Months later, I needed to use the service. After searching through my email, I found a welcome letter that refreshed my memory and got me started, including:

- How to log on (and how to reset a forgotten password)
- Links to getting-started materials and tutorials
- A link to frequently asked questions

Better yet, the email was written in a conversational, friendly style and reminded me why I had signed up for the service. The welcome email can play a critical role for people (like me) who sign up and then wait before taking action.

Another great welcome example comes from Buffer, the social media sharing and scheduling service. Once I signed up for Buffer's "Awesome" plan, two emails arrived right away.

The first, from the account of cofounder and CEO Joel Gascoigne, welcomed me as a subscriber, setting a personal tone for the ongoing relationship. He also reminded me that *I could cancel at any time.* Few businesses do that when you first sign up. Simply seeing that statement increased my trust in Buffer.

The second email was a payment receipt, but here too, Buffer made the transaction fun and personal, including a picture of the Buffer team at a work retreat. The email ended with this quote: "We will also do our best to provide great value for you day in and day out."

Remember what I said about the job of subscription marketing: earning trust and nurturing value? In its two welcome emails, Buffer declared its intention of doing both. Well done.

Video is another great way to welcome new subscribers, since it gives your business a personal face from the start. Seeing an actual person in the video fosters a human connection, which is a great way to start a relationship.

Automated emails and online onboarding are great, but sometimes the best welcome is personal. The more high-tech your solution, the more powerful a personal connection can be—through email, a phone call, a personalized video, or even a handwritten note.

Reduce Barriers to the First Steps

Customer success advocates speak of the 90/10 rule for customer adoption: If a customer doesn't start using your solution within 90 days, there's only a 10 percent chance they'll become a loyal customer. While the precise numbers may vary for your business, the general concept holds true for nearly all subscriptions. If people don't take action quickly, they may forget why they subscribed.

A solid customer launch plan gets subscribers started, so they realize the value of their subscription right away.

Your launch plan might start with a series of emails with links to videos, commonly requested advice, or other useful resources. What's the first thing you'd like a new customer to do: Set up a profile? Order a sample? Think of the smallest step and package it in a customer launch plan.

Automated Onboarding Programs

Technology makes it possible to see what your customers are doing with your solutions and spot whether they're off to a good start. When operating at scale, find ways to automatically track usage and adoption. If it looks like the customer isn't succeeding, reach out and see if you can help.

Test the onboarding carefully, with people both inside and outside the company.

If you want to see examples of the good, bad, and ugly of user onboarding, check the "teardowns" published by Samuel Hulick on his site, useronboard.com. I guarantee you will learn something and return to look at your own onboarding process with fresh eyes.

Chapter 7

Orchestrate Early Success

The high-end dining business is built on repeat customers and customer referrals. A pricey restaurant cannot succeed unless its customers think that the food and overall experience are worth the investment.

Few restaurants in America have the cachet of The French Laundry in Yountville, California. It boasts three Michelin stars and measures its wait list in months.

Once you walk in the door for your long-awaited reservation, the staff hands you a tiny appetizer that looks like an ice cream cone, made with smoked salmon and crème fraîche in a delicate wafer.

I haven't been to The French Laundry (*yet*, that is—I am an optimist) but I have heard the chef, Thomas Keller, discuss the role of his famous "salmon cornet." He calls it one of the most important parts of the meal.

The unexpected and whimsical appetizer serves two functions:

1. The gesture welcomes those diners who may feel intimidated about entering this well-known dining mecca. What better way to break the ice than to give someone a treat that looks like an ice cream cone?
2. The appetizer launches the dining experience with familiar reference points. As Keller says, it tastes like something people have experienced before (salmon and sour cream), so they tend to like it.

From a marketing perspective, this gesture is a customer launch plan rolled up neatly in a wafer: Establish the relationship through a friendly gesture and create the first experience of success.

Look for ways to implant similar early successes with your own solutions.

Use Videos to Accelerate Success

If your solution isn't intuitive to use, marketing should make it painless for customers to get up to speed quickly.

Video can save the day. It's usually easier to *show* customers how to do something than it is to explain it. People can watch videos on their own schedules. Even for relatively easy-to-use solutions, video answers early questions quickly.

Your customers are accustomed to turning to YouTube to figure out how to fix things or learn new skills. YouTube is the second-largest search engine in the world, after Google. According to a study by Pew Research, over half of U.S.-based YouTube users turn to the site to figure out how to do things they haven't done before. Video is a natural choice for initial customer welcomes.

Bonus: If you do a great job creating an instructional video about your solution, it serves two purposes: helping new customers find success and attracting prospects who would be a good fit.

Embed Guidance in the Solution

Even the simplest solutions have a learning curve. Help customers navigate that curve quickly, reaching the point at which being a customer is easy and rewarding without requiring cognitive effort.

Slack is an enterprise messaging and collaboration program that has shifted perceptions about what "enterprise software" looks like by focusing exclusively, even obsessively, on the user experience. From its earliest days, the people at Slack understood that rapid user success was key to its growth. What good is a collaboration tool if you're the only one on your team using it?

In an interview with Kara Swisher on the *Recode Decode* podcast, Slack CEO Stewart Butterfield said that customer success was the company's prime engineering objective: "We focused all of our effort on the new user experience, and I think that's what's made the difference."

This focus carries all the way to the initial login. Instead of an ordinary email confirmation with instructions for logging in, the company sends first-time subscribers a "magic link" to make the initial login painless. A cheerful, automated Slackbot helps people with the next steps and offers context-appropriate options, advice, and encouragement.

If software is part of your solution, consider embedding online guides and pop-up help to direct people through the learning process. Don't go overboard with embedded help, though. Remember Clippy, the helpful paper clip in an earlier version of Microsoft Office? Poor Clippy inspired violent thoughts in Microsoft users worldwide. There's a fine line between offering assistance and intruding. Remember to provide an easy way to opt out.

Today's automated helpers are much more sophisticated than Clippy; artificial intelligence can power chatbots that deliver customized answers on demand while responding like real people.

You don't have to build a bot; you could embed tips and suggestions that show up the first few times someone logs in. Or create a timed email campaign that sends weekly suggestions for the first few weeks after someone subscribes.

Guide Customers Through Critical Milestones

Have you ever started watching a television series on Netflix and found it takes a few episodes before you get hooked? (That's one reason streaming services automatically queue up the next episode, by the way.) Some shows take two or three episodes to pull you in, while others grab you right away. You might bail on a show after one episode, only to retry it when your friends tell you they love it.

Robert Skrob calls this a *retention point* in his excellent book of the same name. Your job is to help your new subscribers reach their individual retention points quickly.

Customer success professionals talk about a metric called Time to First Value (TTFV), which is how long it takes before a new subscriber or customer realizes value. You can use this metric to track how effective your onboarding process is, or whether you're acquiring the right customers. Depending on the complexity of your offering, the customer onboarding process may involve leading customers through multiple steps. Those customers who complete all the milestones will most likely achieve their desired outcomes.

A welcome mail for an online video-editing service invited me to sign up for a walkthrough webinar, which the company holds several times a week at different times of the day. And I was grateful. My learning curve was steep, and the introductory webinar helped me achieve my goals quickly.

The more complex the offering, the more urgent it is for you to guide people from the moment they sign up. If it is complex enough, you may need to supplement the early onboarding with training.

If you've done the work of segmenting customers, you can enroll them automatically in campaigns that lead them through the relevant milestones. If you aren't sure which track a customer should be on, proactively offer them the chance to enroll in the start-up plan that meets their objectives. Flesh it out with training, checklists, and personal assistance where required.

The work you invest in orchestrating the initial customer path pays off in subscribers who remain loyal.

Chapter 8

Help Customers Create New Habits

Does your solution require people to change their behavior? If so, you can influence customers as they shape new habits.

As director of the Behavior Design Lab at Stanford University, BJ Fogg researches how to use technology to change behavior. The Fogg Behavior Model suggests that a behavior is the product of three factors:

1. Motivation: Does the person *want* to do the behavior?
2. Ability: The easier the behavior, the greater the chance of it becoming habit.
3. Prompt: Something must trigger the action.

Identify the specific customer behavior you want to encourage, then figure out how to add the motivation, ability, and prompt. Technology can aid with habit formation by providing a trigger or prompt for these behaviors.

Behavior can be stubborn, and you should not assume subscribers will immediately change the way they do things, no matter how wonderful your solution is.

Guide New Customers Through the Habit Change

Meditation is like exercise; making the time to do it each day is a challenge. For the online meditation app Headspace, the challenge isn't explaining how to use the app; it's getting people to make the time to meditate regularly.

Headspace eases potential customers into the meditation habit by offering a free course of ten days, ten minutes each. Once you subscribe, the company sends a welcome letter with useful links and instructions, encouraging you to complete the ten days. At the conclusion, emails prompt you to continue with a paid subscription and additional meditation courses. You can opt in to meditation reminders or ask to be connected with a meditation buddy.

Getting the reminders right is a delicate balance. As a business promoting mindfulness and inner peace, the last thing the company wants to do is to irritate its subscribers. By guiding customers through the start of a meditation practice and supplementing the software with reminders and social support, Headspace influences habit formation.

Or, for a less esoteric topic, how about driving habits?

My husband and I bought a new car this past year. The salesperson at our local Subaru dealership showed us how to access all the features when we picked up the vehicle, but it's quite a lot to take in. Two days later, as I tried to remember how to work the adaptive cruise control while driving on the freeway, I hit a few stray buttons before I got it set up.

Subaru and its dealers want us to join the ranks of long-term, happy customers. They scheduled a follow-up appointment two weeks later to go over those features again, offering a twenty-dollar gas card as an incentive for us to return.

The follow-up meeting wasn't an upsell for a service contract or other features. A friendly, non-salesy young man led us through everything on the dashboard, showed us his favorite way to set up the various displays, and answered our questions. It was fast and informative, and now I know how to use that adaptive cruise control—it's become a habit.

Habits take a while to form; compress the time by creating incentives and removing barriers.

Encourage New Habits with Gamification

A little friendly competition can serve as additional motivation when forming new habits. That's why fitness trackers suggest that you share your data with others and include competitive and game-like features.

Gamification is adding elements of traditional games (points or badges, competition) to other activities, making them more fun or habit-forming. Many businesses use gamification to encourage adoption and loyalty.

For years, I carpooled to chorus rehearsals in San Francisco with three other singers. Being Silicon Valley denizens, we relied heavily on navigation applications like Waze. As we sat in traffic or wound our way through back streets in San

Francisco, my carpool companions would monitor our progress, keeping track of the changing arrival time, and reporting slowdowns and accidents back to the app. Reporting observed incidents earned the Waze users commuting points that eventually led them to achieve *ninja* status.

For Waze (now part of Google), customers who share their real-time experiences make the data itself richer and more valuable for all Waze users. It's the *network effect* in action, in which each addition to the network increases its value overall. Providing points for participation encouraged the Waze subscribers to use the app, delivering more data and increasing loyalty.

If gamification can improve the experience of commuting in traffic, then it's on to something.

From a value-nurturing perspective, adding a competitive or gaming component may encourage customers to use your solution so that they realize value quickly.

Chapter 9

Offer Great Training

Training programs represent a golden opportunity for marketing organizations to influence the customer's experience of value. Remember that Economic Value to the Customer, or EVC, is the sum of the tangible and intangible values perceived by the customer. For complex products, effective instruction is one of the surest ways to increase the tangible value of your solution. If they know how to use it, they'll have better results, and thus experience the solution's value.

Interestingly, effective training can also move the needle on the *perceived*, or intangible, value. As customers invest time and effort in learning, their personal commitment to your solution increases.

If you do a terrific job of teaching them, people are more likely to become loyal customers.

Choose Training Based on Customer Needs

People have different learning styles and schedules. Design and present the training in the right formats and doses to match the customer's needs.

For example, in the business software world, administrators or power users may seek out intensive instruction, while everyone else can get by with a few videos. You may develop several training tracks, divided into short, functional components that people can access at the right moment in time. If you offer live webinars, publish the recording afterward for those who cannot make the scheduled time.

We are surrounded with diverse options for on-demand learning and instruction in our personal lives; your customers will expect you to provide a similar range of options. Offer training through multiple formats, such as videos, podcasts, and written materials. For directed or assisted training, consider using a learning management system (software designed for online courses). As a bonus, hosting your training on a site like Udemy or Skillshare may create added visibility for prospects.

Add Value through Certification

Amplify the impact of instruction by offering formal certification for customers who complete in-depth training.

Certification gives customers explicit evidence of their skills and makes the solution more valuable as part of their skill set.

Many technology leaders offer certification training, including Apple, IBM, Google, HubSpot, and countless others. Technology companies know that certified practitioners become powerful advocates, particularly in industries in which people change jobs frequently.

Chapter 10

Share Stories

Storytelling is a powerful way to connect with people on an emotional level, to communicate abstract concepts, and to make an impression. We remember stories. We share them with others. As you create content for value-nurturing campaigns, do not forget stories. If you're already creating customer stories, use them to enhance the *perceived value* delivered to existing subscribers.

Share Customer Stories with Your Subscribers

Businesses often rely on case studies or customer success stories as lead-nurturing content to move prospects through the sales cycle. Marketers love them because they create essential *social proof*—the belief that since others are doing something, it must be worthwhile.

You probably already spend time developing customer stories to attract prospects and generate leads. Sending these stories to current subscribers requires little extra effort. Think of this strategy as a free trial of value nurturing, using content you already have at hand.

- When a customer first subscribes, send them relevant stories.

- When you first publish a customer story, share it with existing customers.

- Actively solicit your subscriber base for other examples of great stories or interesting ways people use your solution.

As a member of the discount warehouse Costco, I receive the monthly *Costco Connections* magazine, where the company profiles many of its small business members. In addition to providing useful content, the magazine showcases the members and their activities. Profiling customers is a great way to add value to subscriptions.

Tell the Right Stories

I see a lot of so-called customer stories that suffer from one or more fatal flaws: They aren't actually stories, or they feature the wrong protagonist. (This is particularly true in B2B marketing, where real people become users, personas, roles, or corporate entities.)

Adding a customer name to a data sheet and putting it into three parts labeled Challenge, Purchase Decision, and Results doesn't make it a compelling story. You can find many definitions of what makes a story. Nearly every definition agrees on the following:

A story needs a protagonist whom the reader/listener can identify with.

The protagonist, or hero, should hold our interest. It's hard to get involved in a story when you don't care about anyone in it. The more powerful the connection to the protagonist, the more compelling we find the tale.

Many B2B customer stories choose the wrong protagonist. The two most common protagonist problems are product as hero and brand as hero.

Product as hero. It's tempting to make your own product the hero of the story—the thing that saves the day. Here's an example, with names obscured to protect the brand: "*Productname* Enables *Customer* to Respond to Issues Quickly..." A product isn't a person. As its creator, you may feel a connection to it, but your readers don't.

Brand as hero. Often, you'll find a brand standing in for the protagonist—usually the customer's brand, but sometimes the vendor. (Everyone wants to be the hero.) Please, make the customer the hero of the customer story.

This is harder in the B2B context, when the customer is a business entity. Consider these common headlines and introductions (pulled from real corporate websites):

- *Customer brand* works with *Company* to deploy *Product.*
- *Customer brand* reduces customer support costs using *Product.*

Can you identify with a brand? How about a piece of software? Nope—me neither.

These stories have no human faces, no hero we can root for. The first, and most important, thing to do when writing your customer stories is this:

> Pick the right protagonist and fill your story with people.

Create a Human Connection

Look at your customer stories. Identify the hero of each. Is it your company? Your solution? Your customer's brand? Or is the protagonist a real person (or group of people) solving a real problem?

The best customer success stories follow a specific individual or team, highlighting their challenges and the steps they took to overcome them.

If you're in the B2B area (your subscribers are themselves business organizations), you may not have permission to highlight individuals. Regardless, do whatever you can to make the story human. For example:

- Write a story about a team of people. For example, "The customer support team at Acme had a real problem: not enough hours in the day." The readers you are trying to reach are on similar teams and can probably relate.

- Include personal stories *within* the write-up, from the perspective of a single individual within your business customer's organization who faced a genuine problem before the problem was solved. If you serve the healthcare sector, you could open with a problem faced by a physician at the beginning of the story and describe the resolution at the end. You don't have to name the person as long as you can draw a compelling scenario.

- Interview someone on the customer's executive team. Get quotes from people who took responsibility for the problem and try to get insight into what was at stake. Put a human face and voice on the customer's brand.

Let Customers Tell Their Own Stories

What happens when someone stands up and tells their story, either in person at a conference or virtually via a blog post or customer piece?

By speaking out, those customers become advocates for your business. They internalize and "own" their success as a customer. You've given them a showcase for their expertise and the opportunity to assist others.

Customer stories are one component of *advocacy marketing*, or getting loyal customers to testify on your behalf. Can you think of ways to expand beyond your traditional, marketing-driven "customer success story" program to solicit stories from people in their own words?

The Zendesk blog includes a section labeled "Story Room." In these posts, customers tell their own stories, either through an interview or by directly submitting a written post.

Could you do something similar?

You might dedicate part of the blog for the customer voice or create a customer-only area of a website for people to share their experiences. It could be as simple as an online community or a social media page. Invite customers to share their experiences with others.

Share Your Own Story

Don't just share your customers' stories—understand and tell your own story as well. Remember that when someone subscribes, your business becomes part of *their* story.

Every business has at least one story: an *origin story*. Sometimes it's about the founder, but often it's about a specific situation.

But your story might also be about who or what your business is today, right now. Your *brand story* is all about what you do, and why. It is part of your identity as a business. Bernadette Jiwa describes the importance of having a story that guides your values in her book *Story Driven*. She writes:

> Differentiation happens when you authentically amplify the best of you—discovering how to be more of who you are, rather than finding ways to be a version of the competition.

Used in this sense, telling the right story goes far beyond marketing—it guides business strategy and values at the highest levels. Your story is also a key to your values. (See chapter 19, "Share Your Values.") Make sure that it's authentic and real, and that everyone in the company can get behind it.

This story can live on your website, but it should also inform how you interact with subscribers and the way they feel about being a customer. As Ann Handley writes in her book *Everybody Writes*:

> At its heart, a compelling brand story is a kind of gift that gives your audience a way to connect with you as one person to another, and to view your business as what it is: a living, breathing entity run by real people offering real value.

Remember that a subscription business is based on trust. When you share your story with subscribers, you cultivate trust.

Chapter 11

Quantify Your Value

The fastest way to demonstrate value to a customer is to do the math for them. Put a number on the tangible or intangible benefits of a subscription.

Supermarkets use this technique regularly. When I check out at the local Safeway using a loyalty card, the cashier tells me how much I saved while handing me the receipt, addressing me by name. The transaction includes an *immediate* and *personalized* assessment of the monetary value of subscribing to their loyalty program. (I pay for my subscription to this loyalty program with data, not money.)

We live in a data-driven world, so you probably already have data about your customer usage. Can you use it to nurture your customer's experience of value?

Demonstrate Value with Customer Usage Data

Activity monitors tell us how far we have walked, sleep monitors track how long and how deeply we slept, and the utility company reports on how our gas, electric, or water usage compares to our neighbors. Most of us are comfortable with the concept of usage data at this point.

Chances are that you have data that could reinforce or strengthen your customer's perceived value. Try to convert usage into measures of the benefit to the subscriber: time saved, healthy meals prepared, blog posts published, or whatever is appropriate for your business.

Even if you're already providing that data in reports, guess what? Not everyone runs or reads the reports. Consider making that effort for them on occasion.

If the value that your solution delivers isn't monetary, you may need to be creative to put the data in context or make it interesting.

Many companies send "year-end wrap-up" emails that put usage data in a fresh context. If you use the ride-sharing service Lyft, for example, you receive a year-end report presenting data for the year, including total rides, miles traveled, other stats, and any "badges" that you have unlocked. (The badges are a gamification strategy.) The email can serve as a pleasant reminder of the times you used the service.

Aggregate Value Across All Your Customers

Perhaps you cannot easily pull personalized data for each individual customer. Maybe your service is such that it seems intrusive to deliver personalized data. Anything health related has the potential to be creepy, particular if you're not in the healthcare business.

In these situations, it might be wiser share aggregate data from the customer base rather than individual information.

When using aggregated data, be careful to remove any indicators that would betray individual customer's data or usage.

ThreatMetrix®, part of LexisNexis® Risk Solutions, helps financial and enterprise customers protect online sites and customers from malicious actors. The company publishes a real-time visualization of the fraud attempts detected and blocked across its global network. Circles of varying size and intensity appear on a world map showing the instance and severity of account takeover, payment fraud, and identity spoofing attacks foiled by ThreatMetrix Digital Identity Network. The customers themselves remain anonymous.

Sharing this information demonstrates value to customers and prospects alike. The company also publishes quarterly cybercrime analysis reports for the broader industry.

Whether you're providing individual usage or aggregated data, you'll remind subscribers of the reasons for remaining customers, and perhaps spur them to do more with your solution.

Chapter 12

Celebrate Successes

When I joined my first start-up, it was just a handful of people. The vice president of sales put a small gong on his desk. Whenever we signed a deal, he struck the gong so everyone within earshot knew. In the early days, we were *all* within earshot, since the office was small. As the company grew, the gong-striking celebration continued, setting off minor celebrations and shared congratulations.

Celebrations keep us going through long hauls.

As your business grows, look beyond your own sales for reasons to rejoice. The successes that will fuel your long-term growth belong to *your customers*. The more your customers achieve with your solution, the better for your business. When you take a moment to celebrate with them, you acknowledge and reinforce your partnership.

> When customers experience success with your solution, applaud them without claiming the glory.

Build Celebration into the Experience

Can you engineer celebration into your solution?

MailChimp, the email marketing service, makes it quick and easy to create and send email campaigns. But hitting the Send button on your first email campaign can be nerve-wracking. MailChimp takes the pressure off by showing a giant, animated chimpanzee finger hovering nervously over a button. The moment you send the campaign, the chimp hand gives you a virtual high-five.

It's funny and charming. But it's also an acknowledgment that by sending the mail, you've met one of your goals for using an email marketing solution. The virtual chimp celebrates with you.

Honor Continued Usage

You don't want to be one of those companies that contacts customers only when selling something or raising prices.

A celebration is a great reason to contact a loyal or continuing customer—someone who's not reporting problems and might otherwise be neglected. Look for small victories in customer usage data.

Fitbit sends badges to celebrate certain milestone achievements, such as a maximum number of steps taken in a day, or lifetime distance covered. One day you may receive an email announcing that you have walked the entire length of Italy or India. This serves as a reminder of what you have achieved together. The company doesn't claim the glory. Instead, it celebrates with you.

TripAdvisor occasionally sends me an email reporting how many people have read the reviews I've posted there. It reminds me to write more reviews, but also reinforces the value of those reviews in helping others.

Send Personal Emails

Like many independent authors, I use various Amazon services for publishing my books.

Except for an occasional newsletter, most emails I receive from the Amazon entities (Kindle Direct Publishing, Audible, and more) are transactional in nature, telling me about the status of a draft or shipment. So I was surprised to find a message congratulating me when one of my books was included on a list of the best self-published books of 2016. Someone on Amazon's CreateSpace team took the time to send wishes for continued success. It made me feel like more than an anonymous customer.

This simple gesture of celebration was a powerful example of value nurturing in action.

Chapter 13

Create Value Through Content

Marketers are great at creating content—it's what we do. Great content enhances the value of the solution. It creates value beyond the core product offering.

Supplement your subscription offering with content that customers find useful. You might create blog posts, papers, e-books, social media posts, books, magazines, graphics, podcasts, videos, or other media.

Take the content-marketing strategies you use before the sale and extend them after the customer signs up. Continue to deliver value, and customers will remain engaged. The content has to be valuable in and of itself. Think of ways to serve your customers.

Jay Baer articulates this philosophy beautifully in the book *Youtility: Why Smart Marketing is About Help, Not Hype*: "If you sell something, you make a customer today; if you help someone, you make a customer for life."

Online and Offline Publications

Companies have been creating value through print magazines for decades. Many still find success with this format. AAA publishes a travel magazine (*Via*) as a complement to its insurance and roadside-assistance offerings. Charles Schwab sends an investment magazine to its customers. If your business interacts with customers only intermittently, a content subscription increases loyalty and reinforces value.

A high-quality print publication can become a growth engine, spurring community participation and support. The quarterly magazine *First & Fastest* is a publication of the Shore Line Interurban Historical Society, a group of railroad buffs based in the Indiana/Illinois/Wisconsin tri-state area. Rail enthusiasts beyond the society's Midwestern origins value the quality of the content and print production. The magazine publishes a lengthy list of "sustaining subscribers" who pay more than the baseline subscription fee to support the publication. According to content-marketing expert and *First & Fastest* subscriber Roger C. Parker, "When you deliver exceptional quality on a consistent basis to a targeted market, the support will appear."

While print magazines still serve many subscribers, content distribution is moving online and expanding beyond print. Many brands create online hubs combining posts, graphics, audio files, and videos, offering media for every preference. These sites become preferred destinations for customers looking for more than product information.

Birchbox provides its subscribers with a monthly box of personalized health and beauty product samples. To differentiate itself and add value, Birchbox also publishes an online magazine filled with content related to health and beauty. The site includes articles and instructional videos that help customers get the most value from their subscription boxes. The content goes beyond what's in the box to include author interviews, fashion advice, and stories about taking cosmetics through airport security checkpoints.

As another example, consider Adobe, a company I've already highlighted for its pivot to the subscription model. Adobe runs an online site, CMO.com, for chief marketing officers and marketing professionals. The site's editors curate useful articles, news, and podcasts about marketing and develop original content on trends and predictions.

Adobe does not pitch Adobe Marketing Cloud on the CMO.com site. Instead, the company delivers valuable content for customers as well as prospects. The content hub serves multiple marketing purposes, including brand awareness and value nurturing.

Tune in to Podcasts

Look around you. Those people you see wearing headphones on your commute or at the gym may be listening to podcasts.

According to Edison Research, the number of Americans listening to podcasts has grown rapidly over recent years. (You didn't need me to tell you that, right?) Edison's Podcast Consumer 2019 study found that more than half of Americans over the age of 12 have listened to a podcast. And 54 percent of podcast consumers are open to considering the brands they hear about on podcasts.

If you want to generate content regularly without a great deal of writing, podcasting is one way to go. Better yet, it's got a subscription model built in. A podcast can serve both existing customers and prospects. For it to be effective as a value-nurturing strategy, obey the laws of content marketing by providing information that is useful, educational, or entertaining. Consider creating a podcast series by interviewing people your customers find interesting. Profile customers. Have your in-house experts talk about trends affecting customers or share tips about improving their businesses.

You won't reach all your existing customers with podcasts. There's only so much time in the day to listen to podcasts; you must earn audience attention. But a podcast is a great way to make a personal connection with customers and to repurpose content you share in other formats.

The best podcasts feel like personal conversations, bringing the listener in closer to the brand or strengthening a relationship. Plus, once recorded, podcasts are "evergreen" and continue reaching people with your content.

Turn Data into Valued Content

Many online businesses collect large volumes of operational data. That data may itself be a valuable source of insight for your customers.

The insight you can find in data is nearly endless.

The ride-sharing service Lyft publishes "The Lyftie Awards" for the most visited restaurants, hotels, transit stops, and tourist destinations worldwide, and regional listings for restaurants, bars, and event venues. These awards are a clever way to offer valuable insight based on data that's already been collected as part of doing business.

The search giant Google is awash in data about the searches that happen on its platform. Google shares those insights with the world through Google Trends. Visit Google Trends to see what's trending on search by region in your country. Each year it creates a "Year in Search" post that highlights the biggest search trends of the year, with categories like musicians, recipes, news, and fashion styles.

Subscription management company Zuora mines its subscriber data to identify trends in the Subscription Economy. Because Zuora's customers include more than a thousand businesses that depend heavily on subscriptions, the company has a unique perspective on this trend.

Set a data scientist loose on your data and see if they find insights that would benefit your customers.

Create Entertaining Content

Businesses often use humor to get attention from the world at large and to attract customers. Remember the Old Spice "Smell Like a Man, Man" videos? These funny clips exposed a mature brand to an entirely new demographic. The most entertaining Super Bowl commercials often get more buzz than the game itself.

But humor and entertainment play a serious role after the sale as well, keeping customers and subscribers engaged. Some brands are simply fun to do business with. I open their emails and visit their websites because I know that I will enjoy the experience.

Dollar Shave Club launched its subscription grooming products business with a hilarious video that went viral: "Our Blades are F***ing Great." That video earned the start-up a great deal of attention. Once a subscriber signs up, the barely suitable humor continues with a monthly "Bathroom Minutes" newsletter that accompanies the box and is filled with articles like "Which Body Parts Can You Actually Grow Back?" and others I won't quote here.

Beyond earning attention, being funny can sustain the long-term customer relationship.

Humorous content doesn't belong exclusively to the consumer market. Adobe produced an amusing video in which marketing mishaps delay a rocket launch, as part of its "Do you know what your marketing is doing?" campaign. Humor can work in many markets if it is appropriate for your brand voice.

Alas, being hilarious is easier said than done. You cannot predictably plan to have a campaign go viral. However, you can leave room for humor or a light touch in your customer interactions, like the flight attendants on a Southwest Airlines flight who communicate the safety features of the aircraft with humor. If you can't make people laugh, at least try to make them smile.

Chapter 14

Create Community

Connecting people in meaningful ways is a generous act. While competitors can copy your solution offering, duplicating your community is much more difficult.

Businesses are waking up to the power of community around their solutions. Many software-based subscriptions integrate social commenting, sharing, and messaging to increase the social value of the product. But that's not an option for every type of subscription.

If you can't easily fit social features into your product, the marketing team can create community *outside* the solution.

Build Communities on Social Media

One of the easiest ways to add value to a digital subscription is to create a human community around it on an existing social network. The choice of network will vary based on where your customers hang out.

Business-related software may draw the best participation on LinkedIn, while Facebook groups have proved popular for consumer-focused services. (I cannot count how many writing-related Facebook groups I've encountered.)

Setting up a group is the first step; creating a meaningful community is trickier. Do not use these groups to broadcast brand news; you want to engage and nurture true interaction, while tamping down spam and self-promotion. That's a delicate balance.

With everything else happening on Facebook and LinkedIn, your business presence may get lost in the noise. Earning a place in your subscribers' news feeds can be difficult. You may achieve better visibility and participation by staking out a place in a targeted social media platform.

The Right Margin, a goal-driven writing tool, has found success by carefully building and developing a Slack team dedicated to writers and open to the public, called Writer Hangout.

Like many technology start-ups, The Right Margin used Slack internally to collaborate. The team then created a writing-related team on Slack for writers, existing customers, and beyond. The Writer Hangout team quickly grew to an active, participatory community. The Right Margin team maintains a hands-off approach to Writer Hangout, participating and encouraging without taking over or directing conversations. When customers sign up for the Right Margin service, they receive a welcome email also inviting them to the Slack team.

The Slack community helped the young company reach a broad number of writers early in its lifespan. One thread (or *channel* in Slack terminology) is dedicated to The Right Margin service. This channel serves as a help desk and sounding board for the product teams. The company tests feature ideas, solicits input on potential user interface changes, and gets a better idea of what people want and need through the personal connections forged in the online community.

But this Slack community is not about sales or prospecting. The other Writer Hangout channels cover topics including submissions, rejections, contests, short stories, and book marketing. Many participants make personal connections, communicating through private, direct messages within the platform. The community has become a place where people connect and support one another, which was The Right Margin's purpose from the start.

"We started Writer Hangout as an experiment to see if we could add value to the writing community by using a social channel already so familiar to tech-savvy professionals who were also writers," says Shivani Bhargava, founder and CEO of The Right Margin. "To our surprise, it grew quite naturally. It's been wonderful seeing so many people find and join it organically. What started as an experiment has become its own community and so core to our promise of supporting and motivating writers."

Branded social media communities only work if you commit to participating in and nurturing them, without exploiting them. This means contributing useful content, responding to any service issues, and answering questions promptly.

Create Your Own Virtual Communities

If your community lives on an established social media platform like Facebook or LinkedIn, it is subject to that platform's changing rules and algorithms. Many businesses create and support online communities on their own sites.

American Express has always positioned its customers as *members,* implying a sense of community and exclusivity. When pursuing small business customers, the company goes the extra mile by running its own virtual community, known as OPEN Forum.

OPEN Forum gives American Express members a place to ask questions and share information with other small business owners. Editors post selected articles on technology, leadership, marketing, and finance. The company calls it a forum for *exchanging* advice. This community adds inherent value to the American Express card membership.

Host In-Person Gatherings

Connections formed at in-person events are often stronger than those made online. Salesforce is deeply committed to virtual communities, but it also hosts one of the largest in-person gatherings in the technology industry, the Dreamforce conference. According to the Salesforce blog, over 170,000 people attended the conference in 2019, with an additional 16 million people joining for streaming video.

Salesforce pulls out all the stops at these conferences. Past lineups have included famous musicians, actors, athletes, and business leaders: President Barack Obama, Steph Curry of the Golden State Warriors, the rock band U2, Apple CEO Tim Cook, and more.

Why the major push around a physical conference for a company that prides itself on being entirely cloud-based? Through the in-person conference, Salesforce builds and strengthens relationships with customers and partners. Attendees realize a sense of belonging and community. If the event didn't pay off, I doubt the company would continue to invest in hosting it each year.

On the other hand, if a conference sounds too staid for your business, consider emulating Red Bull.

As a consumer beverage company, Red Bull counts on people repeatedly deciding to buy and drink its product. Each additional purchase is a kind of subscription renewal. (The company also has a subscription magazine—the *Red Bulletin*—so you *can* actually subscribe to Red Bull.)

Many major brands compete for market share in the energy drink business. Red Bull cultivates loyalty by connecting fans with a community, both online and at sporting events. Visit the Events section on the Red Bull website, and you can find an event happening on any weekend, in multiple locations around the world. Samples include:

- Ski and snowboard "open jam" competitions
- Off-road racing and road rallies
- Ice cross downhill racing (this sounds crazy)
- Art fairs
- Music festivals

Red Bull sponsors most of these events, labeling many with the Red Bull brand. Participants and observers become part of the Red Bull community merely by showing up. Customers meet and interact with other people who share their love of extreme sports. How's that for adding value?

Chapter 15

Nurture Your Fans
and Advocates

Loyal customers often refer your business to others. They
talk to the media and analysts when asked and participate in
customer testimonials, providing valuable credibility for your
business.

Advocacy marketing is the practice of nurturing and developing the fans and advocates in your base. Done well,
advocacy marketing is a prime example of value nurturing.
Done poorly, it backfires.

Given their potential value to your business, use caution
when soliciting advocates and customer referrals. In a rush to
build a lengthy list of referrals, businesses can antagonize the
people they most want to nurture.

Your challenge is turning subscribers into fans and fans
into advocates, while sustaining the trust you have earned
and delivering real value to fans and advocates. Marketing

teams and customer success teams work together to develop campaigns and programs to:

- Recognize loyal customers and potential advocates, such as people who proactively reach out with comments or advice for others
- Reward advocacy through recognition, exclusive access, special programs, or simple thanks
- Give advocates the support they need to operate effectively on your behalf

Find Your Fans, Superusers, and Potential Advocates

Evangelists, superusers, advocates, heroes—whatever the label, you want more of them. These loyal subscribers go beyond simply staying and using the solution. They spread the word to others.

> A superuser or advocate is loyal to the point of action.

In the business-to-business context, a superuser may accelerate adoption within a larger account, answering questions for others and demonstrating how the solution applies locally. In the consumer market, your advocates may be those customers who tells friends or influences others.

The trick is finding those people in your customer base who are loyal *to the point of action*. Look for behavior that suggests a loyal fan with a tendency to refer. These may include:

- Subscribers who are active or sophisticated users of the service
- Customers who share recommendations on social media platforms
- People who submit reviews or suggestions for new features
- In the B2B context, individuals in a role that influences a large number of other users

Try to identify loyal fans and advocates through their behavior and reach out proactively.

For example, loyal customers often leave reviews, and leaving reviews correspondingly increases loyalty. Amazon frequently asks you to review products you have purchased from the company. When you submit a review, Amazon thanks you for *helping other customers*. If another shopper marks the review as useful, Amazon lets you know. This is one way of encouraging people who contribute reviews.

In other cases, loyal fans may appear if you create programs to attract them, such as bonus points for referrals.

Adagio Teas uses both approaches, offering opportunities for advocacy and rewarding those they discover. I am a fan of the company's teas and order from them repeatedly. Whenever I place an order, the order page includes social media referral links, which customers can share to earn loyalty points.

One year, I placed an order the day after Christmas. (Emergency holiday tea shortage!) To my surprise, I received the tea the next day. Because I was so delighted with the speedy service, I sent out a tweet. Adagio thanked me (on Twitter) and credited my account with loyalty points.

Notice how this worked. The company monitored Twitter to find my referral. The loyalty points were a gesture of thanks. I did not send the tweet for money or points, but the company rewarded me for my action after the fact.

That leads to my main point, and the place where advocacy programs can go awry:

Advocacy should be earned, not bought.

Reward Advocacy

A company I've never heard of sent me an email recently, offering to pay me for subtly mentioning the company to my email list, without making it seem like an endorsement or advertisement.

I said no.

They were looking for *paid* advocacy, not earned advocacy. The company hadn't earned my trust yet. I trusted them even less when they requested that I not mention to my subscribers that they were paying me.

Paid advocacy raises many sticky issues. In the United States, the Federal Trade Commission has published disclosure guidelines for bloggers and others who promote or endorse products or services in blogs, social media, or advertisements. If you're paid to recommend a product, be honest and say so.

Offering money for referrals or advocacy is a slippery slope for other reasons. It doesn't always make sense from a psychological perspective.

Behavioral psychology reveals that paying people for completing tasks (such as a referral) can actually *reduce* their motivation to act by replacing an intrinsic motivation with an extrinsic one. In his book *Predictably Irrational*, Dan Ariely describes studies in which researchers paid MIT students varying fees to complete puzzles. Ariely found that increasing the monetary compensation *decreased* performance for tasks requiring cognitive skills.

If you are delighted by a service and tell a friend about it, you have done something generous for both the friend and the company. It feels good, and that is your reward. If the company offers to pay you $10 for every friend you tell, the act of referral seems cheapened. The payment puts a dollar value on your action, turning it into a commercial transaction instead of a personal one. This can have several negative side effects:

- You may feel that it's not worth your time. ("Ten bucks? That's all my endorsement is worth?")
- If you refer for money, you lose the satisfaction of acting on someone else's behalf.
- If money is tight, you may refer everyone you know, cheapening the strength of the referral.

You want to encourage customers to refer your business because they are taking a positive action for others, not solely for financial gain.

Money is rarely the best way to incentivize brand advocates and referrers.

Don't underestimate the power of a personal expression of thanks. If a customer has said kind words on social media or referred someone else to your business, take the time to offer thanks, whether through a handwritten note, a follow-up call or visit, or another gesture. Handwritten notes are rare and can make a major impact.

Sending a gift as an unexpected thank-you *after* a referral doesn't pose the same danger as offering payment ahead of time. In the business or government context, check whether the recipient works for an organization with policies against accepting gifts.

Perhaps you can reward the advocate with experiences rather than money. For example, give customer advocates special treatment or access to events they find valuable and interesting.

To scale up your advocacy efforts, create programs to develop, support, and recognize the advocates among your subscribers.

Give Your Superfans and Advocates a Starring Role

A trip to a local brewery recently introduced me to yet another value-nurturing practice: turning fans into participants who improve the product. (Yep, that brewery tour was part of my research for this book!)

Untappd is a social network for beer lovers. Its users track and rate the beers they drink. The avid users visit local breweries and take notes on what they like and the brews on tap. They earn badges for rating beers. So far, this is a classic example of nurturing value through gamification.

But sometimes the app users discover discrepancies in the data and submit it to the site. The most active of those beer-and-data aficionados can become volunteer moderators. In that role, they help maintain and clean the data in the platform.

These individuals are doing the hard and important work of cleaning the site's data. Untappd users apply to become moderators. Having been accepted, their profiles illustrate their elevated status.

We met a moderator on that brewery tour who told us he spends hours every week working on the data. (One hopes he does this before consuming too much beer.) He visits local microbreweries on all of his travels.

The Untappd Moderator Program acknowledges and supports the most avid fans of the platform; they in turn support the platform.

Well-designed advocacy programs benefit everyone:

- The advocates receive recognition, additional resources, and the overall satisfaction of assisting others.
- Newer customers benefit from having experienced people available to answer their questions and provide guidance.
- Your company benefits from increased customer loyalty and success.

How can you put your best customers to work, supporting others or enriching your solutions?

Chapter 16

Loyalty and Membership Programs

Subscription marketing is all about the relationship with your customers. Why not deepen that relationship by inviting customers to become members?

Membership suggests *belonging* and *participation*. Membership extends community, delivering value through a relationship rather than simply goods and services.

When your customers think of themselves as members, they have a tighter emotional connection with your business. They are more invested in its success, and more likely to expand the community. Similarly, when you call people "members" rather than "customers," you recognize that they also have a stake in your success.

Membership is baked into many subscription offerings. For example, you may become a member of AAA, a professional association, a gym, a wine club, or a subscription video service.

A membership program is another way to cultivate a deeper, ongoing relationship with subscribers. What would membership look like to your business? For inspiration on the membership idea, I recommend that you read Robbie Kellman Baxter's excellent book *The Membership Economy*. In her work, Baxter suggests that subscriptions are a pricing model, and membership a mindset. She writes: "The Membership Economy is all about putting the customer at the center of the business model rather than the product or the transaction."

If you're searching for an entry-level membership program you can implement from the marketing organization, look no further than customer loyalty programs.

Loyalty Programs: Not Just for Punch Cards Anymore

The indie bookstore in my old hometown used to have a loyalty card. Each time you bought a book, they stamped it and wrote the value of the book in one of ten boxes on the card. When you'd filled all the boxes, the cashier calculated the average of the purchases and applied it as a discount to your next purchase. This was a time- and labor-intensive way to give loyal customers a 10 percent discount.

I can't tell you how often I arrived at the register only to realize I'd left the loyalty card at home. And I doubt the people working the register enjoyed averaging out book prices while customers queued up at the desk.

The biggest problem, though, was that it was entirely *transactional* in nature. The things I love about that bookstore had *nothing* to do with a discount. I paid more for books at that store than I would have online. I appreciated the store's participation in the community, the knowledgeable and friendly people who worked there, the curated selections and staff suggestions, and the ability to browse the shelves.

None of this was on the card.

Most old-school customer loyalty programs follow this transactional pattern, sometimes adding other perks, like a gift on your birthday. They appeal to the discount-minded and don't necessarily change behaviors or reinforce the unique value of the solution.

A discount is a weak reward for loyalty. If money alone motivates you, you might go elsewhere if you find a better price.

Airline mileage programs used to work the same way, until the upstart carriers offered better fares and pressured the frequent-flyer programs. Now most airlines understand that they need to offer more than a discount and include benefits like early boarding and seat upgrades. They're adding an improved *experience* to the loyalty program.

Can you give your members early access or special content not available to others? Can you elevate their experience? If you want to pull your most loyal customers even closer, think beyond financial terms.

Premium Loyalty Programs Are Changing Retail

What if the loyalty program is itself a revenue-generating product? That's the lesson from retailers like Costco.

A Costco membership gives you access to the deals in the Costco warehouse stores and online. Costco caps its profit margins on goods sold. The benefit it offers members is the resulting cost savings. By limiting profit margins on goods, Costco increases the value of the membership and incentivizes members to shop at Costco and buy more there.

Restoration Hardware offers a membership program for $100 a year; benefits include a 25 percent discount on all full-priced items, as well as concierge service and early access to sales. If you spend more than $400 at Restoration Hardware, becoming a member makes sound financial sense. In the short term, the company will earn less from you if you join only to cut the price of a big-ticket item like a $5,000 dining room table. But paying to join increases your commitment to the company (after all, you have now signed up as a *member*), making it more likely you will visit Restoration Hardware for your next furniture purchase.

Does a premium loyalty program make sense for your business? If so, charge enough for the program to attract the right customers and strengthen their commitment. Focus on the long-term relationship with member, using the membership program to earn and sustain their trust.

Chapter 17

Ask for Advice and Input

Have a new release coming out? Want input on a marketing campaign? Ask your customers for advice, whether for product direction or marketing messaging.

You not only benefit from the insight of your customers, but you'll also strengthen your relationship with people who appreciate being helpful. When someone contributes advice or content to your brand, they form a deeper emotional stake in it.

Customer Advisory Board

Many businesses invite customers to serve on advisory panels, soliciting their opinions about features or services. This is an easy strategy to implement. Ask key customers to serve as your advisors. Then, listen to their advice.

You benefit from the insight and advice of people you identify as either typical or ideal customers. The panel participants develop a stronger sense of loyalty to the brand.

However, this only works if you actually involve the advisors in decisions and listen to their responses.

Customer-Generated Content

Why create marketing content when your customers will do it for you?

I'm being facetious, but some of the most powerful marketing content you create may originate from your subscribers and customers.

From 2006 through 2016, Doritos® ran a "Crash the Super Bowl" ad contest. The company invited people to submit video ads for a Doritos commercial, and the company aired at least one during the Super Bowl. Some were amazing.

You don't need a Super Bowl–sized budget to use this tactic. There are easier, less expensive ways to include customer-generated content in your marketing mix.

Subscription box companies get an enormous boost from the "unboxing" videos that their fans post on social media. (This unboxing phenomenon has created a new type of social media star, the *unboxing influencer*.)

If your subscription box delivers an exceptional experience (anticipation, discovery, and the physical act of unboxing itself), then your fans will share the word and reach others with the same interests.

Babson College asked its community to contribute to a multiyear campaign around the definition of "entrepreneurship." Babson positions itself as the educator for Entrepreneurship of All Kinds™, with business programs for undergraduates, graduate students, and executives. In 2012, the school contacted its community and beyond to crowdsource definitions of entrepreneurship, collecting contributions on a page of its own website.

The school kicked off the campaign using paid media to invite people to participate. Current and prospective students, faculty, politicians, business leaders, and alumni all submitted ideas. The school collected thousands of definitions, which it used to create marketing and branding campaigns.

Inviting community participation extended the school's reach beyond what it could otherwise influence with traditional outbound marketing. The campaign drove more than 200,000 visitors to the Define Babson site, with unique visitors from 182 countries. According to Sarah Sykora, then Babson's Chief Marketing Officer, "We used our limited marketing dollars to engage our community and the market to share our message for us. Their reach is greater than our spending would allow, and third-party sharing is much more powerful than us talking about ourselves."

Let Customers Participate in the Product

Adagio, my favorite tea brand, invites customers to create their own tea blends from the company's teas. You can try your hand at becoming a master tea blender: choosing the teas and percentages, naming the blend, and preparing cover art for the packaging.

The "Fandom" section of the tea blend website includes series tea blends created to honor video games (Zelda's Tea

Chest), *Game of Thrones* (Game of Tea), *Doctor Who*, and more. The tea creator's names appear alongside the tea blends.

Not only does Adagio gain more loyalty from tea enthusiasts who want to express their creativity in blending, they also gain insight into their customers' interests and passions.

How can you open up parts of your product to your subscribers?

Chapter 18

Handle Breakups Gracefully

When you look back at any experience, two things shape your recollection of it: the most intense part of the experience, and the ending. Psychologists call this "peak-end theory." They have demonstrated it in a variety of situations, including one experiment involving colonoscopies. But, let's not get into those details. Suffice it to say, you should craft the end of the subscriber experience as carefully as the start.

Even in the best of situations, customers leave. Let them go gracefully. Make the departure easy and pleasant, because that experience will color their perception of your business.

Former subscribers may remain influencers, recommenders, or more. They might even return, if you handle the departure well and their circumstances change. Don't waste goodwill by trying to squeeze an extra couple months of payments out of them.

The marketing organization should write the end-of-life plan for customers; leaving this moment to chance is risky.

Keep the Exits Visible

We've all heard horror stories about people struggling to cancel subscriptions. Worries about ugly breakups can prevent prospects from subscribing in the first place.

Whatever you do, don't hide the Unsubscribe button. It's the wrong thing to do. Don't make people "call to cancel" so you can try to persuade them on the phone.

Not only is it creepy to hide the exits, it's also illegal in some places. For example, in California, if you automatically renew a subscription, you must give the subscriber a way to cancel that subscription online.

Stop Clinging

Do you tire of the endless "We want you back" emails? Or do you dread the phone call with an agent who attempts to counter every reason you have for leaving? (I had a negative experience trying to cancel a cable subscription when I moved.)

It's *creepy* to cling to a customer who's trying to leave. Find out why they're unsubscribing and try to address any problems. But then let them go with dignity.

When you raise prices, you will lose subscribers. Again, make it easy for them to leave. Netflix did this beautifully in an email announcing a price increase. It explained the price increase and included a link to unsubscribe *in the email.*

If a customer chooses to leave due to a price increase, don't annoy them further by making them jump through extra hoops. Be respectful—they'll remember that.

You might proactively contact inactive subscribers and offer them a chance to leave. I loved the "invitation to unsubscribe" email I received from Return Path, experts in email deliverability and optimization. After asking me politely if I wanted to continue receiving their emails, the message offered me a simple choice: Click on the happy koala to stay, or the sad monkey to leave.

Return Path unsubscribe image

Welcome Returning Customers

What happens when you resubscribe to a business you've left?

- Most businesses treat you like a new customer. You probably aren't insulted, but you do feel forgotten.
- You may be pleasantly surprised if the business welcomes you back and acknowledges the past relationship.
- A few customer-centric subscription businesses let you make up for lost time or pick up where you were before you left.

This third approach promotes ongoing loyalty from intermittent customers.

If a former customer restarts a subscription, welcome that person back like an old friend. Don't make them start at the beginning. For example, create a welcome-back campaign with content that varies based on how long they've been gone. Think about what returning subscribers need and guide them to rapid re-entry.

My son Mark introduced me to the value-nurturing activities of Blizzard Entertainment, makers of the World of Warcraft®, Diablo®, and StarCraft® games. Mark was an avid gamer in high school but stopped playing in college. (Cue the parental sigh of relief.) On summer breaks, he would drop back into the online games.

Many gamers probably follow this pattern; bursts of active use followed by periods with less time for gaming. Blizzard makes it easy to rejoin the gaming world if you've been gone for a while. When you leave, your account is frozen rather than deleted. If you sign up after an absence, the company connects you with resources that help you start having fun quickly, including:

- A Returning Players Guide: The online guide includes account management, major game changes, new features, and the latest updates so that returning players can discover what's happened in the online world during their absence.

- Character-level boosts: The company uses the occasion of new releases (expansions) in the online world to offer incentives for preordering, such as the "level

90 boost" which shortcuts the hard work of "leveling up" a character in the world. These incentives often lure back inactive users.

These resources get the returning player engaged and playing again as quickly as possible.

Chapter 19

Share Your Values

As the world changes, businesses of all types feel compelled to weigh in on issues outside of their direct operations. They're being asked to take a stand for something. That brings us to the final meaning of the word *value* in value nurturing: "principle or standard of behavior."

In addition to demonstrating the value of your solution, can you find connections between your values and those of your customers?

Aligning your business with your customers' values is a powerful business strategy that serves many purposes:

- *Differentiation*: In commoditized industries like electronics or beverages, your business can stand *out* by standing *for* something greater.
- *Employee attraction and retention*: A global survey by the job and recruiting website Glassdoor found that for over half of respondents, company culture is more

important to job satisfaction than salary. Nearly three-quarters of the 5,000 respondents say they won't apply for a job unless the company's values line up with their personal values.

- *Media attention*: The business headlines are filled with stories of businesses taking stances on newsworthy issues. From a public relations standpoint, you might earn more media placement from taking a stance on a hot topic than you could purchase in advertising.

- *Customer loyalty*: When I share Patagonia's commitment to the environment and a responsible supply chain, I am less tempted by that inexpensive winter coat made in China and sold at a steep discount in a big box store.

For subscription marketers, the most important benefit of sharing values may be *earning trust*. We are more likely to enter into an ongoing subscription relationship with businesses that share our values.

> Successful subscription relationships require ongoing trust.

The Rise of Values-Based Marketing

For businesses, taking a stand used to be simple: You could donate goods or services to causes relevant to your brand. That's still one path. But recent years have seen a significant increase in brands taking up issues that are larger than the business itself. Whether you call it ethical marketing or values-based marketing, it's a growing trend.

The 2019 Edelman Trust Barometer shows a significant rise in the number of people who believe that businesses (CEOs), should lead positive change. In the 2019 research, 76 percent of respondents say that CEOs should take the lead on change related to issues of equal pay, discrimination, the environment, and more. This number is up 11 points from the previous year.

Many people now *expect* businesses to take a stance on important issues.

There's a downside. Sometimes, it seems as though brands are cynically appropriating movements in order to earn free press or make a quick buck. These attempts may get media attention, but not of the positive kind. Even honest attempts backfire, earning ridicule or contempt from the very communities the campaign was striving to support.

As a value-nurturing strategy, aligning with customers' deeper values has incredible power. But doing it well is trickier than it may seem and requires commitment well beyond the marketing team. Let's take a quick look at the risks and rewards of aligning your business messaging and behavior with customers' values.

Choose Your Values

Choose the right values on which to base your marketing campaigns and, ideally, business behavior.

The most powerful stories and values align closely with the core business.

Here's a classic example: Dawn dishwashing liquid prides itself on cutting through grease on dirty dishes. It's also effective at cutting through oil on marine mammals and seabirds. For decades, Dawn has donated dishwashing liquid to The Marine Mammal Center and International Bird Rescue for cleaning wildlife affected by oil spills. It publishes videos of volunteers washing ducklings with Dawn dish soap. Who doesn't love baby ducks? In supporting an environmental cause, Dawn reinforces its brand identity and solution value.

What values are core to your brand's purpose?

Although consumers increasingly *want* businesses to take a stand on important issues, there are limits to their tolerance for values-based messaging. People are most receptive to values-based marketing when it aligns with a brand's operations or core purpose.

The Global Strategy Group conducts an opinion poll every year about business and politics. Their Sixth Annual Business and Politics Study identified the issues consumers think are appropriate for brand engagement: fair labor standards, hiring military veterans, diversity and inclusion, the environment, and climate change.

What do these issues have in common? They relate directly to business operations or customer and employee welfare. If the issue is in your brand's wheelhouse, most people think it's legitimate for you to take a stance.

Software giant SAP offers free online courses on sustainability through its OpenSAP online training platform. (I took the course in 2014; it was fascinating.) Thousands of people worldwide take the courses and learn strategies for monitoring, reporting, and minimizing the environmental impact of their manufacturing operations. By affecting the behavior of its customers, SAP multiplies the impact of its environmental and social sustainability efforts. (The company's customers include most of the world's large manufacturers.) Through this effort, SAP reinforces its role as a partner in innovation and supply chain accountability.

Both Dawn and SAP chose campaigns aligned with their solutions and stories. Their values-based actions are tightly integrated with the brands themselves.

However, the Business and Politics survey respondents were less accepting of brands speaking out on hot-button topics, including LGBT equality, transgender issues, immigration reform, marijuana legalization, and support (or not) for the president.

When addressing these hot-button issues, separate the underlying values from the politics and make the connection to your core brand mission.

Highlights for Children has been publishing content for children around the world for over seventy years. You might even think it's a stodgy brand. Yet in June 2019, the company's CEO, Kent Johnson, issued a strong statement denouncing the way immigrant children were being treated at the U.S. border. Johnson also defended the company's right and obligation to speak out.

> "Our company's core belief, stated each month in *Highlights* magazine, is that 'Children are the world's most important people.' This is a belief about ALL children."

He made the strong connection to the brand's mission: Highlights isn't about publishing, it's about children.

If you take a strong stand on political or societal issues far outside your core business purpose, understand the potential risks and benefits.

Privately owned fast-food chain Chick-fil-A has become associated with anti-LGBTQ causes when the chain's founder, S. Truett Cathy, publicly waded into the same-sex marriage debate in 2012. Cathy died in 2016, but his family and the company's foundation continue donating to causes that the progressive news site ThinkProgress identifies as being anti-LGBTQ.

On the other end of the spectrum, Penzeys Spices founder and CEO Bill Penzey sent his customers an email after the 2016 U.S. presidential election, criticizing President Trump's divisiveness. The company launched a variety of "Choose Love" gift packages. In the fall of 2019, Penzeys donated revenues from product sales to raise money for a pro-impeachment ad campaign.

Bill Penzey is unwilling to separate his political beliefs from his business. In an interview with the *Milwaukee Journal Sentinel*, Penzey said that he realized the effort might alienate some customers. "Probably, we'll pick up 1 percent new customers and we'll lose a half percent." He didn't take the stand for a business reason.

For both Penzeys Spices and Chick-fil-A, taking a controversial stance has generated press coverage the businesses could not have bought. It has also cost them customers, while increasing loyalty among others. It's tough to quantify the impact. However, Chick-fil-A's first restaurant in the United Kingdom opened amid protest, and the store's landlord decided not to extend the lease beyond the six-month pilot period.

Chick-fil-A and Penzeys Spices are privately owned, and the values espoused are those of their founders. Publicly traded brands can also wade into explicitly political issues that affect their business, employees, or customer base.

Salesforce and Twitter both have corporate headquarters in downtown San Francisco. Marc Benioff, CEO of Salesforce, campaigned in favor of a San Francisco tax measure that would tax the city's technology companies to fund services for the homeless. Salesforce donated to the campaign. Twitter CEO Jack Dorsey campaigned against it. While customers and others might take sides in the public debate, no one questioned their right to take a stance.

Values-Based Marketing Requires Commitment

Obviously, corporate values must extend far beyond the marketing organization. In the best-known, often-cited examples of values-based businesses, the commitment starts with the CEO.

Patagonia's founder, climber Yvon Chouinard, shaped the company's commitment to the environment. Patagonia makes headlines by encouraging its customers *not* to buy its jackets unless they really need them. That's a revolutionary stance for a retailer.

Patagonia treats its customers like subscribers, prolonging the customer relationship to reduce its environmental impact. The company repairs items that customers bring to the stores. Customers can trade gear that is still in good condition, which will be resold as used through the Worn Wear® program. This program highlights the durability of Patagonia goods. Patagonia recycles any clothing and gear that cannot be resold, keeping those materials out of landfills.

From the CEO through marketing, retail operations, outlet stores, and gear repair staff, everyone at Patagonia is committed to protecting the environment. In 2018, the company changed its mission statement to this: "We're in business to save our home planet." How's that for a commitment to the environment?

While CEO engagement is important, nearly every business can act on issues that its customers and employees care about.

Invite Customers to Participate

Take this strategy a step farther by helping your subscribers act on their values.

The Airbnb Open Homes project offers one example. When disasters strike and floods or wildfires displace people from their homes, the Airbnb Open Homes program empowers the Airbnb community to contribute by opening their homes or rental properties to evacuees and relief workers, as well as refugees from violence and people needing a place to stay during medical treatments.

Open Homes provides the screenings and guest verification and reduces risk by offering reimbursements for any property damage.

This isn't marketing—it's action. But as a marketing strategy, it aligns with the Airbnb mission of hospitality and home, and it strengthens the brand's ties with its community of hosts.

Live Your Values

Genuine corporate values rarely originate in the marketing department. The authentic values resonate with your leaders, employees, and customers.

The best marketing campaign will eventually hurt you if your business isn't genuinely committed to both the story and values you profess.

Make sure you have high-level buy-in for any values-based strategies you deploy.

Otherwise, you'll open yourself up to accusations of *woke-washing*, *virtue-signaling*, pandering, or plain old hypocrisy. Remember BP's "Beyond Petroleum" campaign? BP's relatively minor alternative energy investments were overshadowed by the company's aggressive efforts pursuing oil reserves. Critics accused the company of *greenwashing*, or claiming environmental values they did not follow.

Even well-intentioned but clumsy values-based campaigns can engender ridicule. Dove has practiced effective values-based marketing with its long-standing "Real Women, Real Beauty" campaign focused on challenging conventional norms of beauty. This campaign started in 2004 and earned admiration and attention over the years with creative advertising campaigns.

In 2017, the brand had a hiccup. To celebrate a diversity of body images, Dove came out with different body shapes for its plastic bottles: Real Beauty Bottles. Some loyal Dove customers felt offended by the shapes. The Twitter backlash was instant (and amusing).

While your brand may endure ridicule for a misstep, the backlash can be stronger if people perceive that you are jumping on a values bandwagon for purely financial purposes, such as profiting from a disaster.

> The values you espouse must run deeper than the marketing campaign.

People are watching. Customers and analysts are watching. If you're counting on getting press from your efforts, the press and media will watch and evaluate. If you're jumping onto an existing movement, the leaders of that movement are watching, too.

Your own *employees* may call you out as well.

Consider the cautionary tale of the online furniture retailer Wayfair. On a section titled Our Promise, Wayfair's website states: "Wayfair believes everyone should live in a home they love."

In late June 2019, hundreds of the company's Boston employees walked out to protest that the company was selling furniture to a facility for "unaccompanied minors" in Texas. The business transaction seemed to violate the brand promise by profiting from immigrant children being detained and separated from their parents at the U.S./Mexico border.

No matter how you feel about the policies or the company's behavior, the lesson here is unambiguous: Your employees care about your values as much or more than your customers do. They may speak up when you don't honor those values.

Risks to Marketing Using Deeper Values

Aligning your marketing with customers' values requires finesse and integrity. Whether you're taking a stance on a divisive issue or jumping on to a bandwagon, be aware of the risks. We've already talked about the obvious risks: damage to the brand via negative press, and loss of customers.

Others are harder to detect, including long-term marketing complacency and damage to the movement you hope to support.

Complacency

If you are too successful at values-based marketing, you might fall prey to the *curse of purpose*. This happens when you weight social or environmental virtues more heavily than your core customers do, while neglecting other customer values and requirements.

All things being equal, people want to do business with companies that share their values. This doesn't give you permission to ignore quality, functionality, or price. Whole Foods may sell organic food, but its customers don't sacrifice shopping experience or product quality. Since acquiring Whole Foods, Amazon has also been resetting prices.

Even if you lead with environmental or societal values, that message should *enhance* rather than replace the solution value.

Damage to the movement

When you incorporate a social cause in your brand marketing, you risk not only your brand image, but possibly the cause you hope to support.

This insight comes from Katie Martell, known as an "unapologetic marketing truth-teller" and creator of the book and documentary *Pandermonium*. She suggests that movements like Black Lives Matter or women's equality can be harmed by brands jumping in with one-day campaigns or rainbow flags.

Martell says, "On the surface, it seems like a good thing if brands elevate the discussion to a national level. The flip-side is that these brand campaigns may create an illusion of progress or a sense of normalcy around the issue, when it's not yet reality. This disconnect grows larger as more brands jump on the bandwagon, but the issues themselves aren't addressed."

To mitigate this risk, back up the marketing campaign with genuine action. Again, values-based marketing does not begin and end in the marketing organization. It must permeate the business operations. That's why you choose your values with care.

Three Guidelines

If values-based marketing sounds tricky, that's because it is. Katie Martell offers these three guidelines:

1. *Think twice.* Understand how your stated values line up with your customers' values and your business mission. Does your cause make sense? How will people feel about your campaign? Is the management team on board? And can you run this campaign authentically? Says Martell, "If you're going to run a feminist campaign around International Women's Day, take a look at how you treat women in your own organization first. Do you have implicit bias training? What's your pay equality situation? Think twice."

2. *Practice what you preach.* Remember that we live in a world of radical transparency—people are watching. Taking a stance may affect the short-term decisions you make later.

3. *Think beyond the hashtag.* Consider the effect of your campaign in the real world, beyond clicks and sign-ups. Are you trivializing a larger issue? What can you do beyond the campaign to make a difference?

Values-based marketing doesn't make sense for every business; it depends in part on the customers you serve, and in part on the authentic nature of your business and its people. For some businesses, value alignment is built into the fabric of the business model itself. That's the topic of the next chapter.

Chapter 20

Embed Values in Your Business Model

When it comes to aligning with customer values, the strongest positions belong to those companies that embed a greater purpose in the business model itself. Values and business become inseparable.

You can embed purpose into your products or services, the way you sell them, or the legal structure of the business.

Products with a Purpose

Toms Shoes built its business with the vision of providing shoes to children in need around the world. According to the company story, Blake Mycoskie saw children in rural Argentina going barefoot and wanted to do something about that situation. He started Toms with the premise that for every pair of shoes sold, the company would donate a pair to a child.

Through the Toms One for One® model, the company has given over 95 million pairs of shoes. Every customer participates directly in the company's story through the very act of being a customer. As Toms expanded beyond shoes, it added other donations, such as pairing prescription glasses and optical care with purchases of sunglasses, and clean drinking water with coffee purchases.

In 2019, Toms adjusted its Buy-One, Give-One model to offer customers a choice about which causes they support with their purchase, with "Pick Your Shoes. Pick Your Stand." With every purchase, customers can direct the donation to a cause important to them. Issues include ending gun violence, equality, mental health, homelessness, and safe drinking water. (Giving shoes to those in need remains an option.)

The company's mission and purpose enrich the value of the products they sell. As a customer, you don't simply buy shoes; you buy the knowledge that as you wear the shoes, you've also taken a stand on an issue that matters to you. The shoes are more than shoes.

What if you're working with an established business not built around a mission? You can embed purpose into existing offerings.

During flu season, Walgreens promotes its Get a Shot. Give a Shot® campaign. When a customer buys a vaccination at Walgreens, the company donates money to provide vaccines to children in developing countries, working through the United Nations Foundation.

The Walgreens example is proof you need not be a scrappy start-up to integrate purpose into the fabric of your business model.

These examples aren't subscription businesses, but nothing is preventing you from fitting this approach into your own business model. Think creatively. For example, if you offer a subscription box of children's books, consider changing your business model to donate a book to a school in need for every box you ship.

Redefining the Purpose of the Corporation

A growing number of companies are embracing the concept of the *triple bottom line*, which encompasses people, planet, and profits. Businesses that embrace social and environmental purposes earn a serious competitive advantage by aligning with customers' deeper values. As Simon Mainwaring says in *We First: How Brands and Consumers Use Social Media to Build a Better World:* "The future of profit is purpose: Consumers want a better world, not just better widgets."

Customers want to make a difference with their choices, and they want the brands they choose to help them. According to Accenture Research's fourteenth annual Consumer Pulse Research, two-thirds of the global consumers surveyed wanted to do business with brands that shared their values.

Some people argue that purpose and business don't mix. In publicly traded businesses, management and board members have a fiduciary responsibility to protect the interests of shareholders. With public markets pressuring businesses for short-term, quarterly performance, the profit motive can lead to decisions with negative long-term consequences.

A growing number of businesses counterbalance the profit motive by adopting a legal structure that includes social purpose. These are *benefit corporations*.

In the United States, a benefit corporation is a for-profit entity that includes benefiting the public as part of its legally defined goals. Profit motives are balanced with the public good in making decisions, and the business agrees to report on its stated objectives.

In the United States, state-by-state rules for these entities vary. Around the world, countries are considering or adopting their own versions of benefit corporations.

A nonprofit organization, The B Lab, certifies businesses based on social and environmental performance, public transparency, and accountability. As of mid-2019, the list of Certified B Corporations™ included over 3,000 companies in 64 countries. These are profit-based businesses working to make a difference in the world.

Companies that are just getting started may have an easier time incorporating as a benefit corporation, so the list of Certified B Corporations skews to smaller businesses. But established brands have also adopted the model, including Ben & Jerry's (a subsidiary of Unilever), Patagonia, fashion brand Eileen Fisher, and New Belgium Brewing.

Even publicly traded businesses are questioning the ongoing worship of shareholder value as the most important business metric. The Business Roundtable is a nonprofit association consisting of CEOs of major US corporation like

3M, Amazon, American Express, Coca-Cola, IBM, and more. In 2019, the Business Roundtable issued a statement saying that the real purpose of a corporation extends beyond driving short-term value for shareholders. The statement includes commitments to deliver value to customers and invest in employees.

Consumers, members, subscribers—whatever label we wear, we care about the values of those organizations we support with our money.

When purpose is embedded in the legal business structure, as with benefit corporations, it withstands changes of management at the board or executive level. Customers who do business with B Corporations know that something larger than a profit motive informs the relationship.

The B Corporation movement is expanding, and I expect its continued growth in coming years, particularly as the subscription trend continues to gain hold and ongoing customer relationships become ever more vital to business viability.

Chapter 21

Nurture Free Trial Users

The free trial is a critical part of the sales process for many subscription businesses. Trials give the prospective customer an opportunity to try a solution before signing up.

The trial isn't just about what's in the box or part of the solution. It's also about the experience.

> A free trial is a chance to evaluate the experience of being a customer.

When selling a subscription solution, marketing organizations have two key objectives: demonstrating value and earning trust. Many of the value-nurturing strategies in this part of the book involve demonstrating or adding value. But do not neglect the importance of earning the customer's trust.

Before undertaking a long-term relationship with your business, prospective subscribers want to know they can trust you. They will ask themselves questions like these:

- Is your business going to stick around once they've invested in working with you?
- How careful will you be with their data?
- Can they trust you with automated payments?
- Will they find more success in their personal lives or jobs by subscribing?

The free trial is a test of your ability to earn and maintain customer trust. However, organizational issues can get in the way of these objectives.

The Free Trial No-Man's-Land

The free trial customer is not completely a prospect, nor entirely a customer, but a little of both. That dichotomy leads to problems. For example: Who owns the trial user relationship? How much do you interact with that prospect? What will those interactions look like?

Some businesses take a hard-sell approach to the trial: The sales and marketing team engages under full steam, and the trial customer experiences the electronic equivalent of the used-car sales experience, with persistent emails, phone calls, or chat boxes popping up.

Other businesses adopt a "hands-off" approach, treating trial users like customers, assuming anyone having a problem will contact customer support. Or they hand off customers to customer success teams for onboarding as if they were paying customers.

But the trial user is not necessarily the same as a new customer—not yet.

People often sign up for a free trial before they are ready to make a purchase. They might use the free trial to learn more before committing. The customer success teams should not have to shoulder the burden of following through on the marketing message at this stage.

If you've read this far and believe in value nurturing, then you recognize this important fact:

> The free trial is when lead nurturing becomes value nurturing.

Apply the concepts of value nurturing to help trial customers achieve an early success. Call on the strategies described in this section, and work with sales, support, and customer success teams to nurture the trial subscribers. For example:

- Provide training resources, videos, or email campaigns to encourage trial customers to discover the features that will provide the most value. (If you have segmented your customers, you'll have a better idea of where to steer the prospect.)

- Observe online behavior and trigger campaigns, emails, or phone calls if trial users appear to be lost or off-track.

- Offer assistance periodically (but not with annoying insistence) during the trial.

Remember, the trial is an opportunity to earn the prospect's trust and demonstrate what this relationship will be like going forward. Don't nag and annoy, but be ready and responsive.

Free Trial vs. Freemium

Take care not to confuse a free trial with a freemium (short for "free/premium") model.

With a free trial, prospects can use the solution for a fixed time, then they are expected to convert to a paid subscription or depart.

A free trial may last anywhere from a month to a year or more. The Subaru that I purchased recently comes from the dealer with a subscription to the Starlink system, which includes multiple tiers of services. Honestly, we might not have subscribed, but the dealer automatically included a three-year trial of the "Safety Plus" level of the subscription. Not three months—three *years*. After three years of enjoying the extra safety features, we're likely to renew.

Three years sounds like a long time, but here's a fun fact: According to research from iSeeCars, original owners of Subarus keep their cars on average *eight and a half years* before selling them. Taking the long view makes sense.

Businesses using a freemium model expect that many customers will remain unpaid subscribers, while a smaller percentage will upgrade to a paid offering immediately, and others eventually convert as their needs grow.

If you execute a freemium model successfully, those free users amplify your marketing reach. They will be so delighted with the free version that they become advocates, recommending your service to others. For example, the Evernote application captures and shares online notes across devices. The application grew rapidly through avid fans of the free version of the software; it appears everywhere on bloggers' lists of favorite productivity tools. The customers of the free version became the application's most outspoken advocates.

The freemium model can be a wonderful growth strategy, but it requires careful planning. Remember, your overall goals as a subscription marketer are to demonstrate value and earn trust. For the freemium model to achieve these goals, the following must be true:

1. The free version has sufficient value. It should not be a "gutted" version designed to get everyone to convert.

2. The paid and free versions are different enough that the value of the paid version is evident.

3. You know how many paid users it takes to support the overall platform.

4. The model is financially sustainable, so you do not have to back out features or capabilities from the free version because you cannot afford to deliver them. Once people become used to a feature, they are unhappy to lose it. Entitlement takes hold quickly! Removing features or functions from existing users violates their trust.

The Moment of Conversion

If all goes well, many trial users will convert to paying customers. But not all will, even for the most effective trials. Your optimal conversion rate may depend on how well you target your marketing.

Never assume a trial user will convert to a paid subscription. The way that you handle the conversion to a paying customer can either add to or detract from the customer's experience.

For example, many businesses collect a credit card number at the start of a trial and bill it after thirty days. This approach has many benefits: It filters out the prospects who aren't serious and simplifies the conversion when it does happen.

But when the moment comes that you are ready to bill the customer the first time, do you post the charges? Or do you remind them? Even if you have the customer's financial information or first payment in hand, observe the moment of conversion with care. Surprises at this point are generally not welcome.

If the customer has forgotten about the trial and discovers an unexpected charge on a credit card, you've just eroded trust from the relationship. That does not bode well for long-term loyalty. In 2019, MasterCard changed its rules to prevent vendors from automatically enrolling and billing customers at the end of a free trial; other card providers may do something similar.

I use the Rainmaker Platform to run my author website. When I signed up for the free trial, I gave the company my credit card number.

During the thirty-day trial period, Rainmaker provided a huge amount of training in various formats, including videos, written guides, webinars, and guided tours. The company did not try to "sell" me once. When I had a question, the support team answered it promptly.

Three days before the end of the trial, the company sent me an email that began: "We're writing because in about 72 hours, your trial access to Rainmaker will be ending and your first payment will be processed."

The email included links to login information and additional resources. It also offered individual assistance if needed. But here's the most important thing: By reminding me of the pending conversion, the company gave me implicit permission to cancel the payment if I wasn't happy or ready. By doing so, the company earned my trust—trust reinforced over the long term.

The trial was a terrific model of the ongoing customer experience.

There's a postscript to this story: I so enjoyed the experience of being a customer that here I am, recommending the product to others. Value nurturing done well leads to loyalty and customer advocacy.

Part Three

Putting
the Strategies
into Action

Chapter 22

Subscription Marketing in the Mature Business

If you're part of a large, well-established organization, you have the advantages of product maturity, large budgets, an existing customer base, and more. The biggest barrier to effective subscription marketing may be the status quo. Existing practices and beliefs can inhibit change, including:

- Distinct customer handoffs between groups, or disagreement over ownership of the customer relationship
- Incentive systems and metrics that value the quick win/new sale over long-term retention and customer lifetime value
- Ingrained cultural perceptions that the marketing relationship ends at the point of sale
- A history of chasing short-term growth over long-term results

If you hope to integrate subscription marketing and value nurturing in an established organization, you must address the cultural and organizational challenges. Most of all, you'll need high-level agreement with this strategy.

In this chapter, we'll look at a few of the key issues to address:

- Tracking the right metrics
- Building support outside the marketing organization
- Expanding marketing's reach
- Changing the culture to support subscription relationships

Track the Right Metrics

The word *nurturing* sounds like something that only a liberal arts major would love. But you can justify it using cold, hard numbers.

When building a business case for value nurturing, find out if your business tracks these metrics:

- Customer retention
- Customer (or revenue) churn rate
- Average revenue per account (ARPA)
- Average customer lifetime value

Any of these metrics can create a compelling business case for implementing subscription marketing practices.

Customer retention and **customer churn** are two sides of the same coin. Retention refers to the percentage of customers who renew and stay, while churn refers to the percentage who unsubscribe or don't renew.

Churn can apply to revenues as well as customers. The two types of churn are linked, but not equivalent. If your customers go through hard times and scale back their subscriptions, they remain but revenue drops. If your customers love what you do so much that they upgrade or buy other services, the increase in revenues can offset the loss of other subscribers who aren't as good a fit.

Most businesses have a natural churn rate: customers leave for ordinary reasons having nothing to do with the business. For example, subscribers to a diaper delivery service churn when the blessed day arrives that the child stops using diapers. Any churn above and beyond that natural rate represents lost revenue. That's where value nurturing pays for itself.

Because retention and churn compound over time, relatively small, incremental improvements result in major revenue differences. Think of it like cumulative interest in a retirement account; small percentage changes make a huge difference compounded over decades.

Customer Lifetime Value: How much is a customer worth in revenue to your business over time? What would happen to your revenues if you increased average customer lifetime value by 5 or 10 percent?

In general, a customer's lifetime value depends on three variables:

1. *Spending:* How much the customer spends each period (monthly, yearly)
2. *Margin:* How much is left after the cost of serving that customer each period
3. *Churn:* The probability of the customer leaving

Effective value nurturing increases customer lifetime value by reducing the likelihood of churn and, potentially, increasing spending. Delighted subscribers are more likely to either upgrade or purchase other services from your business.

Use these metrics to shore up your business case as you build support for value nurturing outside of the marketing organization.

Build Cross-Department Support

If you've been paying attention up to this point, you may think that the word *marketing* in this book's title is misleading. Helping customers realize success requires participation and cooperation from many groups in the business, including sales, billing/account setup, operations, consulting, training, shipping, customer success teams, and customer support.

To paraphrase the famous line from the movie *Jaws*, "We're going to need a bigger marketing boat."

The core practices of value nurturing extend beyond the marketing organization. Marketers need to collaborate with customer success teams and other parts of the organization. Everyone is responsible for the customer experience.

From the customer's perspective, your business is a single organization. Yes, customers realize that many people work there, and that they interact with different individuals for billing, fulfillment, or support. Employees may sign emails with their own names.

Yet somehow customers expect consistency.

Think of your own experience. Are you annoyed when you get inconsistent answers from two people at the same company? Or have you ever felt a subtle shift in the relationship from the period before the sale to the days and weeks afterward? Are your calls returned or emails answered as promptly? Does the story remain the same?

> Organizational boundaries are the enemies of the subscriber experience.

As a customer yourself, what is your gut reaction when you experience a disconnect or hear conflicting stories from different groups? Do you think, *They must be suffering from inter-departmental communication issues?*

Probably not. More likely, you think, *That company is ripping me off,* or *They're not very competent—I wonder whether I can trust them.*

Many of us spring to the worst possible conclusion first, unless the business has earned the benefit of the doubt.

> Every missed handoff damages trust.

As you implement subscription marketing practices, connect across teams.

If your business has one, the customer success management (CSM) organization is the first place to visit in your quest to implement value-nurturing strategies.

The discipline of customer success management has grown rapidly in recent years, particularly in B2B and software businesses. It often integrates functions of marketing, sales, professional services, training, and support.

Individual customer success managers often work with small groups of accounts to offer personalized support. To operate at scale, customer success teams deploy traditional marketing techniques.

Irit Eizips is Chief Executive Officer for CSM Practice, a consulting firm that works with customer success teams. She says, "When you have tens of thousands of subscribers, you cannot possibly hire enough CSMs to affect adoption or advocacy in a personalized, high-touch way. You need someone with marketing chops."

Customer success and marketing teams can collaborate along many dimensions of the subscriber experience:

- Identifying and promoting successful use cases among the subscriber base
- Identifying and supporting potential advocates among customers
- Surveying customers about usage and perceived value
- Creating email-based "playbooks" for feature or solution adoption
- Sending automated emails to mark milestones in the customer journey, such as completing onboarding

Eizips suggests that CSM and marketing teams synchronize their mailings to customers. "Customers who are bombarded with messages from both teams may get *email fatigue* and unsubscribe from email communications from your company. In addition, we also found that customers tend to unsubscribe when receiving long surveys. Having customers unsubscribe from email campaigns limits the CSM team's ability to operate at scale."

Collaboration benefits everyone: The CSM remains the primary contact for the customer, and customers are more likely to open, read, and act on the emails that come from a person they know. For example, Eizips has found that webinar invitations sent directly from a CSM's email address lead to higher open rates and webinar attendance.

Expand Marketing's Reach

Here are a few ways that forward-thinking companies are creating the structural foundations for ongoing value nurturing and subscription success.

Embedding marketers in other groups

In wartime, embedded reporters carry the news of what's happening on the front lines to the world at large. In the battle for customer loyalty and advocacy, an embedded marketer can go beyond reporting, playing an active role in gathering customer feedback and generating customer success stories.

Embedded marketers in customer success teams can create proactive, "low-touch" campaigns that align with marketing messages to enable customer success activities across large subscriber bases.

Cross-reporting

If marketing and customer success reside in separate branches of the organization, building collaborative efforts will be difficult.

Some businesses address this issue by creating a revenue-focused C-level role, the Chief Revenue Officer. In a subscription-based business, customer success wields a major impact on overall revenue and would probably land in this domain.

Have someone on the customer success team participate in marketing team meetings and initiatives; this strengthens the links between teams, creating a culture of nurturing customers after the sale.

Customer-focused incentives

The fastest way to institute structural change is by examining the incentive structure. Incentives are a strong statement of corporate culture and values. If you reward marketing teams based exclusively on net new sales, then that's what they will focus on, to the exclusion of existing customers.

Consider aligning performance incentives and measures with the customer experience rather than department-specific metrics. For example:

- Sales compensation linked to how long a customer remains subscribed
- Marketing performance judged not only on net new sales but also customer loyalty and retention
- CSM incentives based on overall customer retention and advocacy, beyond their specific accounts

Work with your teams to determine an effective incentive structure for your business. Focus on goals that represent the customer experience and reinforce, rather than discourage, cross-department collaboration.

Create cross-functional teams for specific purposes

No one wants to belong to another committee or have another meeting. But for the subscriber's sake, you may have to create a new team. Because the customer experience spans many parts of the organization, people from different groups should be involved. If you don't want to set up a perpetual, regular group, convene teams around specific objectives relevant to value nurturing, including:

- Onboarding or customer welcome plans
- New feature rollouts
- Voice of the customer/customer feedback

Shadow colleagues in another department

This could occur as part of a new employee training: Have a marketing hire spend a week alongside a customer success manager, a week in sales, and a week in fulfillment to get a broader sense of the subscriber issues and experience. It need not be a week; a few hours a day might suffice.

Put every employee through the rotation at least once, and schedule refreshers if the business environment changes.

Invite colleagues to your meetings

If you're implementing a value-nurturing initiative that would benefit from the insight of customer success, support, or sales teams, invite them to weigh in *early* during the planning process. Asking them to sign off at the end, without input early on, can exacerbate any communication problems.

Focus on Culture

Successful subscription marketing requires a relentless focus on the customer. As you nurture advocacy among your customer base, you must also become an advocate for the customer. Revisit Chapter 4, "Cultivate Trust and Value," for inspiration.

Marketing organizations have to become customer advocates as much as marketers.

Sarah E. Brown, a B2B SaaS marketing leader and author, has led Voice of the Customer (VOC) and customer-driven content marketing programs for software companies including Frontleaf (acquired by Zuora), ServiceRocket, BuildingConnected, and Autodesk. She says, "As marketers, we're most often focused on our own business outcomes and galvanizing customers to advocate on our behalf. However, in order to foster the growth of the ongoing relationship, we must also advocate for the customers. We must help them become successful among their stakeholders through every piece of content we create and work together to achieve mutual goals."

Even the location of office fixtures can redirect attention and adjust mindsets. Unbounce is a software platform that creates effective landing pages for marketers. As VP of Customer Success at Unbounce, Ryan Engley is laser-focused on customer experience and retention, and advocates for the customers within the rest of the company. One way he does that is by the clever location of automated customer experience dashboards.

His customer success team installed automated, visual dashboards that display current data about the customer experience in common areas on each floor of the company's headquarters in Vancouver, Canada. The displays show comments and Twitter posts from customers, using bright colors and large fonts to draw the eye. For everyone who works at Unbounce, the customer is present, virtually, in the workplace.

If possible, make the customer-focused culture tangible in workplace every day.

Chapter 23

Start-up Subscription Marketing

"I love the idea of value nurturing. But right now, I've got to focus on growth. We'll add value nurturing later, when we have enough new leads."

This comment came from an entrepreneur launching a subscription box company. When you're starting from near zero, nurturing existing customers seems like a problem for the distant future. But the best time to think about retaining your customers is *before* you've acquired them.

You will never feel like you have enough new leads or customers. *Enough* is a moving target that constantly resets to be slightly more than what you have.

If you want to growth-hack your way to success, work on attracting the right customers from day one. Demonstrate and nurture your customers' perception of value, and they'll do the marketing for you. When your customers become part of your marketing team, growth is the inevitable outcome.

In this chapter, we'll look at the following:

- The start-up advantage
- Value nurturing strategies that play to start-up strengths
- How to use the subscription relationship as your start-up product strategy
- How to embed the concept of successful subscription marketing into your company's culture from the start
- The dangers of chasing growth at all costs

The Start-Up Advantage

Much of the growth of today's Subscription Economy has been driven by start-ups that embedded value nurturing in their businesses from the beginning.

- Slack drove rapid adoption in the enterprise by making it incredibly easy for customers to find success quickly with the product.
- Evernote became a well-loved productivity app using a freemium model, offering product value for free to drive loyalty and paid adoption.
- Birchbox pioneered subscription boxes for beauty supplies by orchestrating early and ongoing success with the products in its boxes through helpful content and extensive personalization.

You probably don't have the marketing budget of the major players in your industry. When it comes to adopting the *mindset* of a subscription marketer, you have many advantages over your entrenched competitors.

Established companies are often hampered by how things "have always been done" or the "best practices" in their industries. Organizational silos put the customer relationship in peril, while entrenched compensation policies may incentivize people for net new sales over attracting the right customers.

As a start-up, you don't have this baggage. You can form meaningful relationships with your earliest customers and learn from them, using those subscription relationships to fuel your growth.

How Will You Nurture Value?

Take another look at the strategies in Part Two of this book and think about how you might build them into your business practices and marketing culture. Several are particularly effective for start-ups focused on growing and sustaining customers.

Add value through content. Master the skills of content marketing; they will help you both attract the first customers and nurture them once they're on board. Great content need not be expensive. A large budget is lovely, but creativity and empathy are available at any budget level. If you can imagine your ideal subscriber's perspective, you can create blog posts, videos, and online content that they'll love.

Add value through community. Build a community around your business, and you'll achieve multiple objectives: nurturing customers, attracting new ones, encouraging word-of-mouth, and even reducing support costs. Most important, you'll be creating value in relationships between people.

Share meaningful stories. Stories form strong connections. Tell your origin story; develop a brand story; share customer stories.

Share your values. Pick a cause and stand up for it; this can help you earn trust and might deliver earned media you could not otherwise afford. Look closely at chapter 19, "Share Your Values," to see if this strategy makes sense for you.

Nurture free trial and freemium customers. Subscription relationships are built on trust and value. If you're a new business, customers don't have enough information yet to trust you. In this situation, a free trial or freemium offering can go a long way toward both establishing trust and demonstrating value.

Subscription Content as a Start-Up Strategy

What if you could launch a business with a strong base of customers already on hand? A growing number of start-ups use subscription content to find their initial customer base and build their first products.

In *Content Inc.,* Joe Pulizzi profiles several businesses that started with subscription content, engaging with and listening to the audience until they understood market needs. Only then did they roll out solutions, whether products or services.

The model worked well for Pulizzi's own start-up, the Content Marketing Institute, and numerous other businesses profiled in the book. (The Content Marketing Institute has since been acquired by UBM Technology Group, but still delivers the same fantastic training, events, and content.)

This is the opposite of running in "stealth mode" for months and then bursting upon the market, you hope, in a blaze of glory. Using the subscription start-up strategy, you first interact with customers in a meaningful way, delivering value through content while you learn from them.

If you're at the start of your business journey, consider building subscription relationships *first*, then figuring out what products best serve those relationships. A strong, positive audience can be a significant competitive advantage for your start-up.

> Competitors might copy your solution offering, but they cannot copy your customer relationships.

Build Value Nurturing into the Culture

Start-ups have the easiest path to successful, long-term subscription relationships, because they do not have to break through organizational divisions that have hardened over the years. You can embed a long-term focus at the start of your business.

In a start-up, everyone wears many hats and gets to know one another, often because offices are so small that you cannot help it. You hear firsthand everything that happens, from crisis to celebration. Immediate, shared goals and close physical proximity make it easier to collaborate across traditional divisional lines and to maintain a shared view of the customer.

But as your business grows, building teams and groups, the turf wars can begin. So, it's best to start with a culture of cooperation between groups and treating your customer right.

You have the chance to bake the mindset into the culture as you grow. Reading this book is a great start. Reinforce culture with the operational realities of your business, such as metrics and payment incentive structures. For example:

- Measure and track customer retention and customer lifetime value. (Make your best guesses in the early days.)
- Don't incentivize people on net new sales alone
- Allocate a marketing budget for value nurturing as well as lead generation

Above all, implant a single-minded focus on the customer's experience of value and maintaining their trust.

If it helps, I've created a short manifesto you can post on your wall. You can also find it on my website: AnneJanzer.com/resources.

The Subscription Marketing Manifesto

I recognize that relationships are the most important competitive differentiator my business can have.

I'm building something for the long haul. Whenever I'm tempted to pursue short-term gains at the expense of my subscribers, I resist.

Instead of focusing only on how quickly I can grow, I look at whether I'm attracting the right subscribers—the ones who get the most value from my business.

I try to add value to every interaction with subscribers—even mundane communications like shipping notices or welcome emails.

I make it easy for subscribers to leave if and when they need to. I don't hide the Unsubscribe button and I am quick to honor requests to unsubscribe.

I *listen* to my subscribers. Although I cannot act on all of their feedback, I acknowledge and thank them for their input.

I spend as much time thinking about how to best serve existing customers as I do about getting new ones.

Chasing Growth at All Costs: The Start-up Affliction

In chasing growth, start-ups often neglect *retention* and its counterpart, *churn*.

Well-funded start-ups face a particular risk, because investors and analysts may demand evidence of rapid growth and market penetration.

If you have investors clamoring for news-worthy growth, you can easily become distracted by "growth-hacking" tactics that increase immediate signups without concern for whether those customers actually stick around.

But churn is the enemy of growth. For every subscriber who leaves, you must find a replacement *before* your new signups represent growth. *Churn*—the loss of either customers or revenue—undermines your investment in growth.

Early success and attention can lull start-ups into carelessness about nurturing existing customers. In a fast-growing start-up with $100,000 in annual revenue, replacing $10,000 lost to churn seems manageable. Your eyes are on the first million, not that $10,000.

As your business grows, replacing subscribers who leave becomes more difficult simply because the numbers increase. When your revenues reach $10 million annually, you would need to find a *million dollars* of new business to replace revenue lost to a 10 percent churn rate. That's just to stay even, not grow—and investors want growth.

If you're serious about growth, get serious about managing churn.

Beware Unsustainable Growth

Tracking the story arc of MoviePass™ was like watching a slow-motion train wreck. I couldn't tear my eyes away.

In case you missed this riveting tale, MoviePass was a subscription service for movie theater tickets. Launched in 2011, the company hit its stride in 2017 when it changed the offer to unlimited movies (at most one a day) for $9.95 a month.

That sounds like an incredible deal, right? Moviegoers thought so, too. At its peak, the company reported having over three million subscribers.

But the deal was too good to be sustainable for the company and its investors. AMC Theaters, for one, was not a fan, and started its own, competitive offering.

By 2018, facing financial pressures, MoviePass reduced the benefits of its pass and instituted blackouts and exceptions. Brian Heater, an editor at TechCrunch, described the situation thus in an article in July 2018:

> It's a lot easier to add features than it is to take them away, and all of those who signed up for the service with the expectation of unfettered movie access for a low monthly fee are starting to feel the sting of reality. It's been a death by a million cuts as the company has fiddled with its pricing structure and moved the goal posts of movie access, while experiencing the occasional outage in order to address ongoing money concerns.

In September 2019, the company shut down the service.

Sustainability was never part of grand strategy. Instead, the company made a bold play to come out strong, grab subscribers to gain market dominance, and *then* figure out how to make money—perhaps by selling data about subscriber's viewing habits.

In contrast, Amazon wasn't profitable for years, but they were reinvesting in the business. MoviePass was investing in acquiring customers looking for a bargain, while losing money on the passes sold. The founders appeared to count on investors with deep pockets keeping it going until some magic moment of victory.

Ultimately, the strategy didn't work. Competitors were circling; others jumped in with their own versions. By dialing back on benefits, the company damaged the trust it had with existing subscribers. Instead of nurturing value, it had to decrease it: value destruction.

> Decreasing the value of your offering reduces trust.

There are lessons here for start-ups pursuing rapid growth:

1. Growth isn't always a good thing if you're losing money with each customer and don't have a solid strategy for turning that around.
2. It's always easier to *add* value than to remove it.

Your business story may require you to change course, scale back, or pivot. Do so carefully; remember that trust is the foundation of your long-term business success in the Subscription Economy. Damage it at your own peril.

If you have to pivot, pay attention to which subscribers you are serving and which you are leaving behind. Being all things to all people is a fool's game. Don't alienate the core group you are building your business to serve.

Chapter 24

Subscription Marketing for Solopreneurs and Small Businesses

What if growth isn't your primary objective?

This chapter is for those intent on crafting a meaningful business and serving a specific, targeted market, without chasing rapid growth.

Legions of small businesses and individuals fit this pattern, including:

- Consultants, speakers, and authors
- Local businesses serving a fixed geographic market
- Solopreneurs (one-person businesses) and small firms

If this describes you, value nurturing should be a core business activity because your long-term success is built on relationships, referrals, and returning clients.

Yet even those of us in this situation are distracted by the siren song of the next new customer, client, or speaking gig. Booking a new opportunity *feels* good—it's rewarding. And so, we may neglect the very people who have sustained and built our businesses.

I first encountered Paul Jarvis when I took his online MailChimp course. Jarvis writes software, teaches online courses, and is the author of the wonderful book *Company of One*. He uses that term to refer to any business that questions growth as its main objective. Jarvis writes:

> Too often businesses forget about their current audience—the people already listening, buying, and engaging. These should be the most important people to your business—far more than anyone you wish you were reaching.

As a participant in the Subscription Economy, "companies of one" have many advantages over larger organizations. Sure, you may not have the budget of the big guys, but you have something that they don't: *yourself*.

The Subscription Economy is kind to solopreneurs and small businesses because it's grounded in long-term relationships, and it's much easier to form a relationship with a person than with a business entity.

As you look through the strategies in Part Two, focus on activities based around *relationships* and *community*, such as:

Sharing stories

Providing value in every transaction or interaction

Celebrating subscribers' successes

Creating content with a personal touch

In this chapter, we'll explore a few ways you can leverage the practices of subscription marketing to build lasting businesses based on value and relationships. Let's start with one activity you're probably already doing: email marketing.

Join the Subscription Economy by Email

Many solopreneurs provide goods or services that don't easily fit a subscription billing model. Perhaps your services lend themselves to individual projects rather than ongoing subscriptions. You might sell a few online courses or derive most of your income from one-time transactions or book royalties.

Find a way to embed subscription relationships into your business right away. Don't worry about linking revenue to the subscription at the outset. Focus on building those subscription relationships instead. If you're not ready to add a membership or subscription offering, consider starting with a simple, non-revenue-producing subscription relationship: the email subscription.

An email subscriber pays you with the currency of attention by giving you permission to send messages and by opening and reading your emails.

Doing email well can be tricky. To see what I mean, look at the "marketing" emails in your inbox right now from a subscription marketing perspective.

Some are spammy; they abuse your trust by trying to sell, sell, and sell.

Others deliver real value. They're informative or funny. Some are welcome reminders of your relationship with the sender. Those are effective value-nurturing emails.

Seth Godin is a prolific author and a genuine thought leader in the marketing space. He emails his subscribers every day. Yes, *every day*. These posts (which live on Seths.blog) are short, but inspiring. By showing up and providing value daily, he earns the right to occasionally tell his subscribers about his latest courses and books.

Why do all this work when there's no revenue tied to it?

If you've read this far, you know one answer: Use emails to *sustain and nurture relationships* with existing and past customers, and future ones.

The discipline of regularly producing content for your audience forces you to put yourself in their shoes, learn about their issues, and empathize with their situations. This makes your future work better, whether you're writing books, coding software, or crafting furniture.

This email list can also be the gateway to subscription revenue. For example, the email content may become part of something bigger, like a book or podcast. Godin's book *What to Do When It's Your Turn (and It's Always Your Turn)* curates and compiles inspirational posts from his blogs in a beautiful package.

Or consider premium email subscriptions. You might offer both free and paid email subscriptions, giving paid subscribers early access, personalized input, or extra content.

People pay for subscription emails that deliver real value. I subscribe to Jane Friedman's every-other-week newsletter on the publishing industry, The Hot Sheet. Friedman compiles and comments on developments in this rapidly changing industry, regularly interviewing publishers and others and tracking the latest data. I look forward to reading it whenever it arrives.

While the revenue from paid subscriptions may be small, the benefits are outsized. For Friedman, publishing The Hot Sheet puts her at the forefront of publishing industry news, and connects her with people in her industry and beyond. It reinforces her core value as someone who understands the publishing industry. She is making a subscription product from the ongoing research she would do anyway.

Even if you're earning revenues, the primary benefit of a subscription email may be the opportunity to forge a closer connection with your audience. People who pay to subscribe to your blog will put aside the time to read the emails more carefully and will contact you with questions or insights.

Whether you offer paid or unpaid subscriptions, choose those value-nurturing activities that let you highlight your personality and core strengths.

Be the Face and Voice of Your Business

Large organizations often struggle to put a human face on the brand. They may rely on spokespeople or talking geckos to personify the brand. They worry about fonts and logos.

You've got something better than a logo—yourself. Don't be afraid to show up as yourself in your business.

Your writing voice

Add value to every interaction with your customers simply by being yourself, even if you rely on automation to simplify your operations.

When someone emails you, respond in person. Send a personal note and write so it reflects who you are.

Don't try to sound like every other brand. Sound like yourself. (But edit. Dear heavens, please edit and revise so you sound like the *best version* of yourself.)

Show your face on video

When this book first came out in 2015, video marketing fell into two camps: cheap and amateurish or expensively produced.

No longer. With the right lighting, your phone or laptop can deliver high-resolution video. Add a decent microphone, and you've got something that looks both professional and personal.

Video is a great way to showcase your human advantage.

Speak up

If you'd rather hide from the camera, you're in luck. You can take advantage of the huge growth in podcasting to make human connections with subscribers and prospects alike.

I could quote a statistic about the growth of podcasts and audiobooks, but it would be out of date before this book reaches your hands. Take my word for it, this channel is growing rapidly. Launch your own podcast or appear on others. There are so many podcasts out in the world that you could easily book yourself on a bunch of them.

When people listen to you on a podcast or audiobook, you are speaking right in their ear. They form a picture of you and feel your presence. They connect with you through your inflections. Listening forms intimate connections.

Do the Things That Cannot Scale

If you want to differentiate your business from larger competitors, think small. Specifically, think about those things that larger organizations cannot or will not do. You can do the things that don't scale, and sometimes small is beautiful.

Answer emails personally

I encourage people on my email lists to send me their writing problems, book recommendations, or suggestions. I even do monthly book drawings where, to enter, my subscribers have to reply to my email.

This gives me a chance to hear from people directly and to connect on a one-to-one basis. (You are invited to let me know what you think of this book. I'll respond, really!)

Ask for advice and input

Chapter 17 discussed the psychological power of asking for advice. This strategy is valuable for individuals and small businesses alike.

When a big brand asks for advice, it sends out a questionnaire. Maybe it runs a focus group. You, however, can take a less scalable approach:

- Schedule a phone call (or better, a video call)
- Meet in person if you're in town

Get creative about your non-scalable activities. In his book, Paul Jarvis profiles Sean D'Souza, a consultant who sends boxes of chocolates to his customers, along with a handwritten note. That would certainly get my attention!

What can you do that's non-scalable, unique to you, and manageable to sustain your long-term relationships?

Chapter 25

Common Challenges and Risks

In the years since the first edition of this book was published, I've interacted with many subscription-based businesses as a subscriber, spectator, fan, and occasionally advisor. Certain patterns repeat themselves, and some are problematic.

As you scan through the following issues, remember this premise: After the initial signup, your core challenges are *sustaining trust* and *nurturing value*. You can damage your business through any actions that betray customer trust or erode value.

Most often, when businesses misstep, it is because they have focused on their own objectives and lost sight of customers' goals. If you sustain trust and nurture value, customers will stick around and help your business grow.

Your business is engaged in a long-term relationship with its subscribers, and everyone knows that relationships are tricky. Some people don't like change and others always demand something from you. Subscription success depends on navigating the needs of those customers while also serving your own business interests.

No one said it would be easy.

Let's start with the most egregious problems: evil intentions toward your subscribers.

Tricking or Trapping Subscribers

Every now and then, I meet people who wrinkle their noses at the thought of subscription marketing, as if encountering something that smells bad.

They've experienced the unethical or lazy businesses that take advantage of their subscribers or hide behind recurring payments. These businesses live in the "dark side" of subscription marketing.

You've either heard about or experienced it yourself:

- The cable subscription you can never cancel
- The record or book club you sign up for and get stuck with for the rest of your life
- The surprise subscription charges you find on your bill for a service that you'd signed up for but entirely forgotten about because the company went silent or you weren't using the service

Some businesses approach the subscription model with the objective of getting as much as possible from unwitting subscribers while they can. They attempt to trick, confuse, or befuddle people into paying for more than they get. In the short term, these companies often make money. Eventually, they lose subscribers' trust. Without sustained trust, a subscription business cannot thrive.

Those negative experiences make the path more difficult for every other subscription business.

If you want your business to stick around, commit to *sustaining value* provided to the customer. Return to the concept of Economic Value to the Customer (EVC), the sum of tangible and intangible value as experienced by the customer. Improving the subscriber's experience ultimately adds value to your solution and, eventually, your business.

Value is not a zero-sum game.

> In a subscription business, customer value begets business value.

The pull of the "dark side" is very strong. Voices in your business or your own head may whisper temptation. Resist!

How do you know if you are trending to the dark side? Here's a major red flag: Do your revenue projections depend on customers making poor decisions, against their own best interests? For example:

- You count on subscribers forgetting that they've signed up, so you're careful not to interact with them around renewal time in case they don't want to renew.

- You base revenue assumptions on the likelihood that people will subscribe for a higher level of service than they actually use.

- You force people into an ongoing subscription when they only need a one-time service and hope they will delay cancellation out of neglect or inertia.

188 Subscription Marketing

- You make subscription and renewal automatic, but cancellation is a difficult, time-consuming effort rife with pushback and arm-twisting.

It's important to spot when this thinking infects your strategy. If *you* detect it, your customers will, too, and they will respond accordingly.

Potential customers and current subscribers have encountered other businesses that try to trick or trap customers. They will compare your practices to those past experiences, looking for signs of malicious intentions. Earning and sustaining their trust will be more difficult.

Assuming that your business model is based on building and delivering value, let's move on to missteps or challenges in execution. From the suspicious subscriber's perspective, even the most innocent of slipups can look like you're switching to the dark side.

Organizational Silos

If I had to pick the single root cause of most subscription execution problems, it would be organizational barriers fracturing the customer's experience.

- A promise made in the marketing or sales cycle doesn't reach the team doing fulfillment.
- A hip, fun, "We care about you" marketing message is followed by a difficult, bureaucratic onboarding or fulfillment process.
- A subscriber in the midst of a serious support problem receives a cheery upsell message.

These disconnects can cause service interruptions or glitches: Subscribers have to repeat themselves or chase problems through accounting and support teams. Severe instances appear in trouble tickets or complaints.

But the smaller hiccups are harder to detect. The customers see these problems, but you may not.

Disconnects and glitches multiply if the marketing organization stops paying attention once someone subscribes. Your business may have multiple, isolated groups talking to customers, with no one tracking the overall experience of the subscriber.

Successful subscription marketers collaborate consistently with those outside their own teams.

Using Customer Data Carelessly

The data you collect from customers is a terrific source for value nurturing. You can deliver usage data to individual customers, or aggregate data and share it with the world.

But remember: Your so-called big data is actually an enormous collection of personal information. Individual behaviors generate that data. Be careful about letting slip any details that violate subscriber privacy.

Customer data dangers include:

- Lax security that lets customer data out into the wild—data breaches
- Inappropriate sharing of individual subscriber information. If you are not diligent about making the data anonymous, you can let slip data that can be traced to

specific individuals. If the data includes financial information that is fodder for identity theft, be extra careful, because hackers can cross-reference their way to actual identities.

Avoid anything that prompts a customer to wonder: *How do they know that about me?* Think carefully before sharing subscriber data with partners and follow local government regulations about using and sharing data.

Before you use subscriber data for anything beyond directly serving or adding value to subscribers, examine your motives. Are you doing it for your corporate fame and glory, or for the subscriber's benefit?

If the worst should happen (like a data breach) despite your best intentions, don't cover it up. Act quickly to regain trust by owning and fixing the problem.

Removing Value from Subscribers

Whenever possible, avoid making changes that customer might perceive as losses.

For example, some companies launch with a freemium model: free service for most people, premium for others. But they have no plan to scale up. The free service users love it and spread the word, leading to rapid growth. Hampered by their own success, the company strips functionality from the free version, assuming that all those happy users will gladly upgrade to a paid version. After all, they've been getting those features without paying so far, right?

Rather than being grateful for the months or years of free use, those formerly happy subscribers feel betrayed and cheated. Many will not upgrade. A few complain loudly on social media about corporate greed.

You might run into a similar problem when trying to change pricing models. I blame *loss aversion*, or our human tendency to fear losses more than we value gains. It doesn't take long for us to feel entitled to something that we've been given for free. When that thing is taken from us, we feel cheated. The pain of the loss colors our judgment.

The morals of this story are twofold:

1. If you choose a freemium model, make sure it's one you can sustain through growth.
2. If you have to change a pricing model or service, try to avoid framing it as a loss. For example, if you raise prices, can you add features simultaneously? Is there a way to present the situation as a potential gain rather than a certain loss? When Amazon increased the price of its Prime membership, it outlined the new value it had added to the subscription. Couple price increases with value increases.

Death by Pricing Complexity

Pricing is one of the trickiest parts of a subscription business.

- The price must sustain the business, offsetting the cost of customer acquisition and covering ongoing service delivery while leaving room for profit.
- The price should reflect the customer expectations for the value delivered from the service (the Economic Value to the Customer)

- Pricing levels also set customer expectations and determine which customers you attract.

Setting your price too low can land you in financial trouble while attracting the bargain-hunter customers who may not renew or who are always shopping for a better deal. Find the price point that attracts those customers who value what you offer and are likely to remain long-term subscribers.

Besides the actual pricing numbers, determine how complex your pricing plan should be. How many tiers or options should you offer?

People like choices. In today's business environment, we want and expect choice in the things we buy. Having choices gives us a sense of control, which makes us happy.

But more is not always better in regard to choices. When presented with many options, we must engage our rational, analytical minds and expend energy figuring out the best option. If you're selling complex enterprise software, for example, that analysis may be part of the sales cycle. You can accelerate the sales cycle by *minimizing* the cognitive effort involved in deciding.

Here's the interesting part: Cognitive science tells us that having *too many* choices often leads to regret. After we make the difficult decision, we are more likely to regret the choice we made. We might rethink it or wonder whether one of the other options was better.

Giving potential customers too many choices is a recipe for creating unhappy customers. We can handle three choices (small, medium, large), but are easily overwhelmed by too many options.

What if your solution is inherently complex? Consider breaking down the decision process into steps with a few options at each phase. Look at Adobe Creative Cloud, which lets you subscribe to bundled or individual applications. The company guides you through the options in a series of easier questions:

- Do you want a bundle or a single app?
- If a single app, which one?

Let prospective subscribers guide themselves, minimizing the cognitive load of deciding and the potential for regret.

The Insensitive Upsell

Has your wallet ever been lost or stolen? It's hard to know what's worse: the fact that someone stole your wallet, or the realization that you have to call the credit card companies. I had this unfortunate experience not long ago, which gave me the opportunity to compare how various banks handled this all-too-common situation.

After I navigated the automated voice recognition menus, all of the banks eventually connected me with a real person. One bank, however, made the situation just a little worse. After I carefully selected the "Report a Stolen Card" voice option, the company first tried to cross-sell me on an unrelated loan program for veterans.

Really?

I'd just told the automated call routing system about a stolen credit card. It doesn't take a psychic to figure out that a customer in this situation isn't receptive to a cross-sell pitch.

Never try to cross-sell an upset, stressed-out, or angry subscriber. Just solve their problem quickly.

Chapter 26

Four Fundamental
Rules of Value Nurturing

To support and nurture customers after the sale, abide by a few basic rules:

1. Value starts with the customer
2. Be human, but consistent
3. Handle mistakes with grace
4. Don't be creepy

These guidelines aren't unique to value nurturing. You probably practice most or all of them today, and we've already covered them in other parts of this book. But with a subscription model, in which you maintain an ongoing relationship with the customer, these rules are not optional. Let's revisit them.

Rule #1: Value Starts with the Customer

Run a quick litmus test on every value-nurturing campaign: Is it about your business or the customer?

To build long-term success, your business must meet your *customers'* needs. A clever video that wins awards and goes viral is meaningless from a value-nurturing perspective unless your customers find it entertaining or useful.

> Value nurturing begins with the customer's perspective.

Particularly in business-to-business industries, marketing organizations spend a great deal of time and money communicating the wondrous features of their solutions. Some technology enthusiasts cannot differentiate between a product feature and its benefit to the customer.

Big brands are accustomed to being the heroes of their own stories. Sometimes you have to cater to stakeholders other than the customer. But don't confuse this with creating content that customers can use.

Value nurturing puts the customer at the center of the story.

In the book *Winning the Story Wars*, Jonah Sachs writes about the long history of "inadequacy marketing," or marketing based on the idea that prospects *lack* something that can be fixed only with a purchase. He writes:

Inadequacy stories encourage immature emotions like greed, vanity, and insecurity by telling us we are incomplete. These stories then offer to remove the discomfort of those emotions with a simple purchase or association with a brand.

With inadequacy marketing, the hero of every story is the product, service, or the brand providing it. We are surrounded by messages that we can be smarter, richer, cooler, or less thirsty if we simply buy the right products.

Sachs contrasts this approach with what he calls "empowerment marketing," or marketing in a way that helps customers on their own paths to growth or maturity. When you practice empowerment marketing, the customer is the hero of your stories. Your solution fills one of many possible roles in the customer's journey, supporting and enabling the customer.

Consider Apple's advertisements that show people doing wonderful or creative things with the iPad. The device is the enabler, while the Apple *customers* are the stars.

Once someone becomes a subscription customer, inadequacy marketing ceases to be effective. If your solution doesn't address a genuine need rather than a manufactured inadequacy, the customer will catch on and stop subscribing. If you rely on empowerment marketing, then your messages continue to resonate with people, urging them to step up into the leading role.

Value nurturing is all about joining and supporting the subscribers on their journeys. If your solution empowers customers, then your business will also succeed.

Rule #2: Be Human, But Consistent

We expect a lot from the organizations we do business with.

On one hand, we understand that every business is a collection of people. As customers, we want to interact with real people when we have a problem or question. Employees may blog or tweet in their own names, and company "About Us" web pages show photos and profile employees to humanize the business.

On the other hand, we also expect consistency across all parts of a business. Whether in a sales or service interaction, we don't want to have to repeat ourselves, or hear mixed or contradictory messages. In this sense, we see businesses as single entities.

Our expectations for both humanity and consistency have implications for marketing in the Subscription Economy. Marketing messages, tone, and style create expectations for interactions beyond the sale. Marketing defines the personality for the overall brand, and the rest of the business must live up to it.

Whatever personality you express, it should be consistent with your business and the people in it. If you cast your business as a caring, values-driven organization, then you must behave in that manner when interacting with customers in all parts of the business, and throughout the entirety of the customer relationship.

One way to ensure consistency is to create a brand style guide and share it throughout the company, not only the marketing organization.

Tone and style extend beyond your written communications to online interactions, phone conversations, and website pages.

For inspiration, check out the error message pages of your favorite brands. IBM's error page, for example, you'll displays their logo in reverse, with "Oops, that's not right!" underneath. On MarketingProfs site, you'll see a confused-looking dog, with the message "Well, this isn't where you wanted to be... is it?" Both then offer helpful links to get you back on track.

Every interaction is an opportunity to reinforce the brand personality and enhance the relationship.

The error page example brings us to the next rule. If "to err is human," then you'd better know how to handle mistakes well.

Rule #3: Handle Mistakes with Grace

In business as in life, when you make a mistake, accept responsibility and make it right.

When you engage honestly with your customers, you get negative feedback that isn't fun to hear. It's a golden opportunity. For every customer with a genuine problem, assume that dozens of others feel the same pain but say nothing. By finding and addressing the pain points, you can make things better for many others. Be grateful to complaining customers, because they're giving you the insight to improve.

When you hear about a problem or make a mistake, deal with it quickly and openly. Social media channels magnify any mistakes, but if you deal with them openly, they disappear eventually. Try to cover up or blame the customer, however, and you'll reach a new level of negative exposure.

In today's highly transparent world, nothing makes your brand look worse than picking a fight with a customer.

One historic hotel in New York City fined its wedding customers $500 if anyone involved with the wedding wrote a negative online review. That's a terrible idea for oh-so-many reasons, and it blew up on social media. (Moral of the story for consumers: Always read the contract before you sign.)

While you can offer a conciliatory gesture to make up for a mistake, beware of offering discounts to keep unhappy customers from leaving. A study by Vamsi Kanuri of University of Notre Dame's Mendoza College of Business and Michelle Andrews from Emory University found that offering discounts to make up for failures in service actually increases churn. Discounts can lower the perceived value of the solution. You're reframing the service as something less expensive.

Better to offer a free month to make up for a service problem than to lower the price.

Rule #4: Don't Be Creepy

When engaging with customers, look for the line dividing personalized from "Big Brother" and creepy. Don't cross that line.

Artificial intelligence powers chatbots that mimic human interactions. Make sure people understand when they're communicating with a real person or with a bot.

Technology and big data deliver real-time insight into customers' online behavior. You can use this insight to create highly targeted campaigns that delight customers. But if you stalk your customers online and interrupt them with messages that demonstrate that you're watching their behavior, some people will feel spooked.

Understand your customers. What delights one might distress another. Where possible, offer people a chance to opt out if they find a campaign intrusive. This is particularly the case if someone visits your website and believes they are anonymous (because they haven't logged on). Be careful about what you communicate unless you have explicitly asked permission to install a cookie or leave them logged on. No one wants to do business with Big Brother.

If you're not sure whether a campaign or idea goes too far, test it with several customers and see if you're hitting their creep factor. What matters is what *they* think, not what you think. As an added bonus, asking for advice is a technique for nurturing value. (See chapter 17, "Ask for Advice and Input.") You may strengthen the customer relationship because you asked.

Chapter 27

Opportunity Awaits

The strategies in this book are based on a central truth: Subscription-based businesses maintain ongoing relationships with their customers far beyond the initial signup. Customer marketing isn't a "nice-to-have" function—it's essential.

For marketers, the challenges of adapting to the subscription trend are many. But I'd argue that there's never been a better time to be in marketing if you want a chance to make a difference in your business. As a marketing professional, you have license to be creative. You can expand your reach, creating value for your business and its customers.

Creativity Needed

The old rules of marketing don't apply; you have permission to make up new ones. When it comes to marketing for subscriptions, everyone is learning on the job, and nobody has all the answers—not even the marketing gurus.

Huge budgets are nice but not necessary. Marketing powerhouses like Coca-Cola and Procter & Gamble face genuine challenges from smaller businesses that understand their markets intimately. Content marketing, social media, and digital marketing level the playing field. Changing business models are creating new platforms for delivering value.

With storytelling as a marketing imperative, creativity is at a premium. As the examples in Part Two illustrate, people who look beyond the usual ways of doing things can make a huge impact with their customers.

Remember, you are participating in a constantly evolving lesson in subscription marketing: Look around and learn.

Filling Bigger Shoes

You may work outside your comfort zone as an advocate for customer value. Step into that challenge. A subscription business model presents marketers with the opportunity to play a larger role, reaching beyond traditional pre-sales activities and influencing the business direction and revenues directly. If that's going to happen, you have to collaborate closely with all parts of the business involved in maintaining the customer relationship.

Many examples in this book extend beyond the marketing organization. The "usual suspects" involved in customer success include customer support and renewal sales or account management teams. You may also work with product designers, training and documentation, operations staff, and others to set and execute on customer expectations.

The broader your reach within your organization, the larger your potential impact on the subscriber's experience.

Increasing Business Value

Marketing is no longer just about getting to the sale. To keep subscription customers renewing and reengaging, you have to provide real value and solve problems. Doing so requires a deep understanding of the customer.

A growing number of people want to know the *values* of the organizations they do business with. The need to strengthen ongoing relationships with customers makes it critical for businesses to understand and claim their *own* values. The good news is that employees of values-driven companies are more engaged at work.

And you just might have more fun.

Changing the World

I'll end this book with my optimistic vision of how the Subscription Economy can make the world a better place.

Let's start with this premise: Successful subscription businesses adopt a long-term perspective toward customer relationships. Thus, the subscription business model weakens the short-term profit focus that drives our current financial system. That's a good thing, because short-term profit motivation can create sustained damage. (Witness environmental damages or the economic crisis of 2008.)

Customer loyalty is critical for subscription success. The most successful subscription businesses will be those with the most loyal customers. So subscription-based businesses have an even stronger incentive than most to align with their customers' values.

Think about the impact of that equation at scale across society. The world economy is incredibly powerful. If it slowly redirects its efforts to the issues people care about, the potential impact is enormous. And that, my friends, is how the Subscription Economy can change the world.

Before You Go

If you're interested in developing and expanding your subscription marketing skills, here are a few things you can do today:

1. Learn from others. Visit AnneJanzer.com/resources to find further recommended reading.
2. Start a discussion group with your colleagues. You'll find a discussion guide in the resources section noted above. Get a few colleagues together and talk about how these practices apply in your work situation.
3. Join my Subscription Marketing group. Sign up on my website to receive monthly email updates from me about subscription marketing, as well as reviews of relevant new books.
4. Leave a review of the book. Reviews help other people find the book. If you like the idea of these practices, spread the word.

Together, we can change the practices of marketing, one business at a time.

Subscription Marketing Manifesto

If you have a subscription or membership component to your business, post this manifesto somewhere prominent, where it reminds you of your long-term objectives.

We recognize that relationships are the most important competitive differentiator our business can have.

We're building something for the long haul. Whenever we're tempted to pursue short-term gains at the expense of subscribers, we resist.

Instead of focusing only on how quickly we can grow, we look at whether we're attracting the right subscribers—the ones who get the most value from the business.

We try to add value to every interaction with subscribers—even mundane communications like shipping notices or welcome emails.

We make it easy for subscribers to leave if and when they need to. We don't hide the Unsubscribe button and we are quick to honor requests to unsubscribe.

We *listen* to our subscribers. Although we cannot act on all of their feedback, we acknowledge and thank them for their input.

We spend as much time thinking about how to best serve existing customers as we do thinking about getting new ones.

Acknowledgments

If were to name everyone who has influenced, guided, and shared with me, the list of people would be at least as long as the book itself. So, please realize that what follows is merely the tip of my gratitude iceberg.

For this third edition, I owe a particular debt of thanks to the people on my Subscription Marketing email list and the readers of earlier editions. Time and again, people have contacted me with stories, suggestions, and insights that have made this book better.

Robbie Kellman Baxter has given me deeper insight into the broader cultural and business model implications of subscriptions, while also offering unfailing support and guidance.

Others have graciously let me share their stories and opinions in this edition, including Katie Martell, Irit Eizips, Sarah E. Brown, Rollis Fontenot III, and Jane Friedman.

This book as it appears before you has benefited from the efforts and advice of many individuals. I'm grateful for Holly Brady's guidance and Laura Duffy's brilliant cover design. Laurie Gibson and Mark Rhynsburger have improved the text with their editorial and proofreading acumen. Any faults that remain are mine alone.

Closer to home, my family has been endlessly patient and supportive through the publication of this book—three times! They have brought me examples of subscription successes, found errors, and provided suggestions to make the book better. I am forever grateful for their love and support.

Research and Notes

For a list of books related to this topic, visit AnneJanzer.com/resources and look for the Subscription Marketing reading list.

If you're interested in learning more about the specific research or examples cited in the text, here are places to look.

Introduction

Find the latest Subscription Economy Index on the Zuora website: www.zuora.com/resources/subscription-economy-index.

I first heard Jill Soley's definition of marketing in her interview on the Marketing Book podcast with Douglas Burdett, before following up directly.

Chapter 1: The Growing Subscription Economy

Did you know there's a patent search in Google? You can find the description of Amazon's anticipatory patent here: patents.google.com/patent/US8615473B2/en.

Chapter 2: Shifting to Subscriptions

The Adobe quote comes from the press release dated May 6, 2013, "Adobe Accelerates Shift to the Cloud." The Adobe revenue numbers in this chapter come from the company's stated financial results.

My source for the data about Prime vs. non-Prime spending is Morgan Stanley's article "Amazon Disruption Symposium:

Where so Far? Where to Next? Who is Safe?" published September 18, 2017.

The Ascend HR case study is based on multiple conversations I've had with Rollis Fontenot III. This is the second time I've profiled his company in this book.

Chapter 3: What This Means for Marketers

The funnel and French horn images in this chapter come from DepositPhoto, used with the standard license.

Chapter 4: Cultivate Trust and Value

The quote at the start of the chapter comes from the book *Fanocracy: Turning Fans into Customers and Customers into Fans* by David Meerman Scott and Reiko Scott, published by Portfolio Penguin in 2020.

Chapter 6: Create a Customer Launch Plans

The welcome email examples come from my own experience. Of course, these emails may have changed if you sign up for these services today.

Chapter 7: Orchestrate Early Success

The French Laundry story is, alas, still hearsay. However, I first heard Thomas Keller discussing the importance of his cornet (the most important part of the meal) on an episode of "Wait Wait... Don't Tell Me!" that aired on July 18, 2014. You can listen to the episode on NPR's website.

The data about people searching YouTube comes from a Pew Research survey of U.S. adults conducted May 29–June 11, 2018.

Check out Robert Skrob's book *Retention Point* for a more detailed description of this concept.

Chapter 8: Help Customers Create New Habits

Find out more about BJ Fogg's Behavior Model on his website at www.bjfogg.com, or in his book *Tiny Habits*.

Chapter 10: Share Stories

The Bernadette Jiwa quote comes from the excellent *Story Driven: You Don't Need to Compete When You Know Who You Are*. You owe it to yourself to read this one.

The Ann Handley quote is from her excellent *Everybody Writes: Your Go-To Guide to Creating Ridiculously Good Content*, used with permission from the author.

Chapter 11: Quantify Your Value

The ThreatMetrix Web Fraud Map is accessible at www.threatmetrix.com/threat-map.

Chapter 13: Create Value Through Content

Jay Baer's quote comes from his excellent book *Youtility: Why Smart Marketing is about Help Not Hype*.

The data about podcasting listener growth is from Edison Research, The Podcast Consumer 2019, available at EdisonResearch.com.

Google Trends can be accessed at trends.google.com. It's fascinating.

Find the hilarious Adobe "launch" marketing video on YouTube: youtu.be/ao7wOJ5qQ-s.

Chapter 14: Create Community

The Right Margin story comes from conversations with Will Sullivan and Shivani Bhargava.

The Dreamforce attendance data can be found on the Salesforce blog.

Chapter 16: Loyalty and Membership Programs

Robbie Kellman Baxter has definitely influenced my thinking about membership. Read her book *The Membership Economy.*

Chapter 17: Ask for Advice and Input

The Babson College story is based on conversations and emails with Sarah Sykora.

Chapter 18: Handle Breakups Gracefully

Daniel Kahneman describes the peak-end theory in his excellent *Thinking, Fast and Slow.*

Chapter 19: Share Your Values

The insight about the importance of values for employee retention comes from a Glassdoor survey. The company described the results in a press release on July 10, 2019: "Culture over Cash? Glassdoor Multi-Country Survey Finds More than Half of Employees Prioritize Workplace Culture Over Salary."

The Edelman Trust Barometer 2019 is the source of the data about people wanting CEOs to take action. Find the latest report on the Edelman website at www.edelman.com.

The Global Strategy Group 2019 study "Doing Business in an Active World: Business and Politics" is available at www.globalstrategygroup.com.

Kent Johnson's tweet about Highlights for Children and children on the border can be found on Twitter: twitter.com/Highlights/status/1143572539358240774.

The interview with Bill Penzey is in an article from the *Milwaukee Journal Sentinel* by Rick Romell on October 15, 2019, "Wisconsin's Penzeys Spices raises another $435,000 for Trump impeachment ads."

For Chick-fil-A's problems in London, see the article "First Chick-fil-A in U.K. to Close in 6 Months Amid Protests," by Derrick Bryston Taylor in the *New York Times* on October 19, 2019.

Chapter 20: Embed Values in Your Business Model

Find the latest data about the Toms donations on the company's impact report, published on its website on the Impact section: toms.com/impact.

Find a summary of Accenture's Consumer Pulse research in the company's press release dated December 5, 2018: "Majority of Consumers Buying from Companies That Take A Stand on Issues They Care About and Ditching Those That Don't, Accenture Study Finds."

Katie Martell was incredibly helpful in gathering content and clarifying ideas for this chapter. Check out her writing on this topic, especially her book *Pandermonium.*

Chapter 21: Nurture Free Trial Users

The research about car loyalty is available on the iSeeCars website.

Chapter 22: Subscription Marketing in the Mature Business

Irit Eizip's quotes and insights come from conversations and emails with Irit.

The Unbounce story is from interviews I conducted with Ryan Engley.

Chapter 23: Start-up Subscription Marketing

You can find many sources for the ongoing MoviePass story. The "peak subscriber" report is from the Helios and Matheson press release dated June 13, 2018: "MoviePass surpasses 3 million paying subscribers." And the wonderful quote from Brian Heater is in his TechCrunch article published less than two months later, on July 31, titled "MoviePass will raise prices to $15 a month while limiting access to blockbuster films."

Chapter 24: Subscription Marketing for Solopreneurs and Small Businesses

If you're not chasing rapid growth, check out Paul Jarvis's book *Company of One*. The quote is used with his permission.

Chapter 26: Four Fundamental Rules of Value Nurturing

The research about the offering discounts for problems comes from the article "Deal or no deal? How discounts for unhappy subscribers can backfire on businesses," by Shannon Roddel, published on Phys.Org on July 1, 2019.

Index

About the Author

Anne Janzer is an award-winning author on a mission to help writers and marketers communicate more effectively.

As a professional writer, she has worked with more than one hundred technology companies. She offers online courses and in-person workshops on writing for marketers and others who communicate about technical topics.

Anne is the author of three other books: *The Writer's Process*, *The Workplace Writer's Process*, and *Writing to Be Understood: What Works and Why*. Her books have won awards from the Independent Publisher Book Awards, Foreword Reviews, Reader's Favorite, and IndieReader.

She contributes to numerous industry publications and blogs, and posts regularly about writing and marketing on her website at AnneJanzer.com.

Connect on Social Media

Website: AnneJanzer.com
Twitter: @AnneJanzer
Facebook: Anne H Janzer
LinkedIn: Anne H Janzer

222 Subscription Marketing

Share Your Thoughts

If you liked the strategies in this book, leave a review (on Amazon, Goodreads, or wherever you may have found the book). Please spread the word.

Made in the USA
Monee, IL
14 March 2021

62715088R00134